HAUNTED TOMBSTONE

HAUNTED TOMBSTONE

CODY POLSTON

Haunted America

Published by Haunted America
A Division of The History Press
Charleston, SC
www.historypress.com

Copyright © 2018 by Cody Polston
All rights reserved

First published 2018

Manufactured in the United States

ISBN 9781467139717

Library of Congress Control Number: 2018942450

Notice: The information in this book is true and complete to the best of our knowledge. It is offered without guarantee on the part of the author or The History Press. The author and The History Press disclaim all liability in connection with the use of this book.

All rights reserved. No part of this book may be reproduced or transmitted in any form whatsoever without prior written permission from the publisher except in the case of brief quotations embodied in critical articles and reviews.

CONTENTS

Preface   7
Introduction   11

1. Big Nose Kate's Saloon   21
2. The Bird Cage Theatre   34
3. Brunckow Cabin   56
4. The Buford House   63
5. The Crystal Palace Saloon   76
6. Boot Hill Graveyard   85
7. Red Buffalo Trading Company   96
8. O.K. Corral   100
9. The Streets of Tombstone   110

Bibliography   121
About the Author   125

Preface

Perhaps you have heard some of the ghost stories of hauntings in Tombstone. Like so many other places in the Wild West with violent histories, Tombstone is said to be one of the most haunted towns in the state.

However, there is a distinct difference between a ghost story and a personal paranormal experience. Usually, ghost stories are nothing more than that, stories. Told with enthusiasm and exhilaration, they are viewed as a form of entertainment and considered acceptable in that way. Each tale has a central character and follows the typical three-act structure indicative of storytelling.

On the other hand, personal experiences usually lack a beginning and end. They are brief personal narratives of some observed phenomenon that often has an element of mystery to the narrator.

These narratives almost always start with a disclaimer and end with the narrator's voice trailing off, followed by yet another disclaimer. They are told reluctantly and with an apology. Personal experiences are often considered to be the delusions of a troubled mind, and the narrators of personal experiences are conscious of the potential for being judged as nonsensical. As a result, they assume a position that anticipates the dismissal of their observations and conclusions.

The narratives contradict some academic assumptions that the belief in ghosts is caused by various kinds of error, impaired reasoning or poor observation on the part of narrators. While this may be true in many cases,

Preface

it is much more complicated than that. Each narrative adds information on the accumulation and determination of evidential criteria. This, in turn, opens up the interpretation of the sum of all the narrative events for discussion. The sense used here is similar to the legal definition from *Bouvier's Law Dictionary*, which defines *evidence* as that which tends to prove or disprove any matter in question or to influence the belief respecting it. Belief is produced by the consideration of something presented to the mind. The issue thus presented, in whatever shape it may come, and through whatever material it is derived, is evidence of a sort, even if it is anecdotal. The goal of this book is to preserve some of these narratives and share some of the fascinating histories of the town "too tough to die." Whether you are reading it for entertainment or using it as a source for research, I hope that you find the information that is presented useful and informative.

There are several individuals I need to acknowledge for their contributions to this book. The first is Rich Donovan and his group, Ghost Patrol with Donovan.

Ghost Patrol with Donovan started in 2001 as a one-off radio show on KRQ in Tucson, Arizona. Rich Donovan worked at KRQ as a DJ and assisted with production for the station. Once it aired, a longtime friend and producer, Polo, suggested that they do the ghost hunts for real. After a lot of investigation and research, Donovan and Polo got in touch with the Southwest Ghost Hunters Association and myself, and they learned the techniques for proper ghost hunting.

Since then, Ghost Patrol with Donovan became more than a one-time show on KRQ. The group has investigated over two hundred different locations. However, they are not paranormal investigators or paranormal specialists. Instead, the team consists of audio specialists, photographers and videographers who have come together with a desire to learn the history and character of the places they have visited. They have a mutual sense of adventure and curiosity for the unknown and created their team of investigators who just want to have fun in some of the area's creepiest locations looking for ghosts and trying to record it on some of today's technology. Ghost Patrol with Donovan is still a radio show, and every year in October, Donovan airs the audio from hunts done throughout the year on 100.9 K101 in Sierra Vista, Arizona. I am still involved with the Ghost Patrol to this day, and Donovan's contributions to the material contained in this book are significant.

Preface

I am also grateful to Joshua Hawley and his team, Tombstone Ghost Hunters. Their insightful investigations of Tombstone's haunted places are a wealth of information and significantly contributed to the accumulated knowledge of the paranormal occurrences that have been reported in the town of Tombstone. Joshua is also an author, and if you like this book, I would highly suggest picking up a copy of his work *Tombstone's Most Haunted*.

Introduction

The lands in southeast Arizona were isolated and among the last to be developed by American settlement. These were the lands of the fierce Apache tribes. After the death of Cochise in 1874, there was no clear succession of leadership. This made the Apache more rapacious and created severe hazards for any settlers who entered the area.

Because of this, when Ed Schieffelin decided to prospect in the San Pedro Valley in 1877, he used Brunckow's Cabin as a base of operations to survey the country. After many months, while working the hills east of the San Pedro River, he found pieces of silver ore in a dry wash on a high plateau called Goose Flats. It took him several more months to locate the source. When he found the vein, he estimated it to be fifty feet long and twelve inches wide. Schieffelin's legal mining claim was sited near Scott Lenox's grave site, and on September 21, 1877, Schieffelin filed his first claim and logically named his stake Tombstone. The name came to mean much more for those notorious and nameless who died there and are laid in Boot Hill.

When the first claims were filed, the initial settlement of tents and wooden shacks was located at Watervale, near the Lucky Cuss mine, with a population of about one hundred. Schieffelin, his brother Al and Richard Gird, their mining engineer partner, eventually brought in two significant strikes, the Toughnut and the Lucky Cuss. Schieffelin also owned a piece of Hank Williams and John Oliver's Grand Central, which they called the Contention. The San Pedro Valley quickly became a mining bonanza.

Introduction

Storefront on West Allen Street, 1933. *Library of Congress.*

Ironically, hard-rock mining was the antithesis of the American western dream, for the minerals required substantial capital and company organization to get the ore out. Former territorial governor Anson P.K. Safford offered to find the financial backing for a cut of the strike, and so the Tombstone Mining and Milling Company was formed to build a stamping mill. While the mill was undergoing construction, U.S. Deputy Mineral Surveyor Solon M. Allis finished surveying the site of the new town, which was made public on March 5, 1879. The tents and shacks near the Lucky Cuss were moved to the new town site on Goose Flats, a mesa above the Toughnut Mine broad enough to hold a growing town. Lots were sold on Allen Street for five dollars each. The town rapidly had some forty cabins and just over one hundred residents. At the town's founding in March 1879, it took its name from Schieffelin's first mining claim. By fall 1879, several thousand souls were living in a canvas and matchstick camp perched above the richest silver strike in the Arizona Territory.

Like all mining towns, Tombstone grew like a mushroom. The mill and mines were continuously running with three shifts; union wages paid $4 a day, and the mostly young, single men needed some place to roar. Allen Street provided it. Nearly 110 locations were licensed to sell liquor, and most sold other things as well. The hotels, saloons, gambling dens, dance halls and brothels were open twenty-four hours a day. By 1881, the population had reached 6,000. At the height of the town's growth in 1885, the community

Introduction

was near 10,000, making it the largest city in the territory. By 1884, the miners had taken $25 million in silver out of the ground. The most considerable difficulty facing the miners was obtaining water. Until 1881, it had to be hauled in. Eventually, the Huachuca Water Company created a pipeline that funneled water twenty-three miles from the Huachuca Mountains.

The rough part of town was situated along Allen Street. All around it, respectable people were struggling to earn a living and establish civilization as they had done elsewhere in the West. Four churches catered to different denominations (Catholic, Episcopalian, Presbyterian and Methodist), and there were two newspapers (the *Nugget* and the *Epitaph*), schools, lodges and lending libraries. Schieffelin Hall, a large, two-story adobe building, provided a stage for plays, operas, revues and all the respectable stage shows. The Bird Cage on Allen Street provided the stage for the disreputable ones.

The town developed a split personality. On the one hand, decent, God-fearing folk trying to make a fair life for their families; on the other existed the flashy, commercial town full of soiled doves and tinhorn gamblers who catered to the wants and desires of the miners and cowhands. In the back of the demimonde lurked a criminal organization that would take a presidential proclamation and the threat of martial law to dislodge. There was also a fundamental conflict over resources and land; traditional, southern-style "small government" agrarianism of the rural cowboys contrasted with northern-style industrial capitalism.

Ruins of commercial buildings on Fremont Street, 1933. *Library of Congress.*

Introduction

In the beginning, Tombstone was part of Pima County, whose seat was in Tucson, many hard miles away. Even farther away was Prescott, the territorial capital. The territory was run by the Democrats, who, in those days, were surprisingly corrupt. In 1881, the southeast corner of Pima County was divided to create Cochise County—with its seat in Tombstone—and the situation in the newly formed county was difficult. Not only were hard cases drawn there by the presence of silver, but the town also was located close enough to the Mexican border to become the center of an extensive trade in stolen cattle.

The head of the Cowboy rustlers was N.H. (Old Man) Clanton. He owned a ranch of sorts near Lewis Springs. The Sulphur Springs Valley was the site of another cattle rustling group, the McLaury brothers. The two groups controlled the water holes for miles around. What cattle they did not run up from Mexico, they lifted from their neighbors. Their hired help and comrades were the likes of Curly Bill Brocius and Johnny Ringo, and only the strongest could hold out against them.

In the summer of 1879, the first ore shipments came out of the mill, and by the fall, the first Wells Fargo stagecoach robbery had occurred.

The Cowboys struck and retired to their ranches, untouchable because they were protected by the corrupt Cochise County sheriff, John Behan. Very few of the Cowboys were ever arrested, even when they had been recognized, and those few unaccountably escaped custody. Old Man Clanton died in 1881, murdered in retaliation for a cattle raid into Mexico, and his place as the gang's leader was taken by Curly Bill Brocius, who had killed Tom White, Tombstone's first town marshal.

Soon, the Cowboys were determined to dominate Tombstone as they did the surrounding countryside. Between them and their objective stood two men: U.S. Deputy Marshal Wyatt Earp and his brother Virgil, the town marshal. Many of the town's honest people banded into a vigilante group called the Citizens Committee of Safety and backed the play of the Earps.

Political and economic factors also brought about the enmity between the two groups. Personal hatred is what brought on the gunfight. On October 25, 1881, Ike Clanton rode into town and got incredibly drunk. He then went from bar to bar, openly threatening to kill the Earps and their friend Doc Holliday. The following morning, he was joined by his brother Billy, Frank and Tom McLaury and Billy Claiborne. The tension in the air was thick, and the townsfolk were uneasy.

It was just after two o'clock in the afternoon when Wyatt, Virgil and Morgan Earp walked out of Hafford's Saloon on the northeast corner of

Introduction

Above: The location of the trial of the Earps and Holliday for murder after the gunfight. *Library of Congress.*

Right: Wyatt Earp before he came to Tombstone. *Wikimedia Commons.*

Introduction

Fourth and Allen Streets to apprehend the Clantons and their comrades for violating the law against carrying firearms within the town limits. As they walked toward the O.K. Corral, they were joined by Doc Holliday, indignant at the thought that they might leave him behind.

The offices of the O.K. Corral were on Allen Street between Third and Fourth, but an empty lot ran through to Fremont Street toward the north. The Cowboys waited in in the open lot between Fly's Photo Studio and the Harwood House. Sheriff Behan rushed to meet the lawmen midway and announced that he had disarmed the Cowboys. After finding that he had not arrested the men, the Earps and Holliday brushed him aside and continued down Fremont Street. As they passed Fly's Studio, they turned left into the yard and confronted the five men. What happened next took only thirty seconds. Seventeen shots were fired on each side. When the smoke finally cleared, Frank and Tom McLaury and Billy Clanton were dead. Virgil and Morgan Earp were wounded, and Doc Holliday was grazed in the hip.

After the gunfight, the Earps moved their families to the Cosmopolitan Hotel for mutual support and protection. When Judge Wells Spicer exonerated the Earps and Holliday of murder, the Cowboys were infuriated and even more determined to get revenge. The reign of terror increased. Mayor John Clum, the editor of the *Epitaph* and a staunch supporter of the Earps, survived an assassination attempt by sheer luck and quick thinking. Murders on the streets of Tombstone and stagecoach robberies increased.

At about 11:30 p.m. on December 28, 1881, three men hid in an unfinished building on Allen Street across from the Crystal Palace Saloon. They ambushed Virgil Earp as he walked from the Oriental Saloon to his room. He was hit in the back and left arm by three loads of double-barreled buckshot. The Crystal Palace Saloon and the Eagle Brewery behind Virgil were struck by a total of nineteen shots. Three passed through the window, and another went about a foot over the heads of several men standing by a faro table.

Because Virgil's arm was permanently crippled by the attack, another town marshal was appointed, and the Earp faction lost important official power because Wyatt's jurisdiction as a U.S. marshal applied only to federal cases.

The *Weekly Arizona Miner* wrote about the repeated threats received by the Earps and others.

> *For some time, the Earps, Doc Holliday, Tom Fitch and others who upheld and defended the Earps in their late trial have received, almost daily,*

Introduction

anonymous letters, warning them to leave town or suffer death, supposed to have been written by friends of the Clanton and McLowry [sic] boys, three of whom the Earps and Holliday killed and little attention was paid to them as they were believed to be idle boasts but the shooting of Virgil Earp last night shows that the men were in earnest.

The *Los Angeles Herald* reported on December 30 that the "Doctor says there are four chances in five that he [Virgil Earp] will die." It stated that "Judge Spicer, Marshal Williams, Wyatt Earp, Rickabaugh, and others are in momentary danger of assassination....The local authorities are doing nothing to capture the assassins so far as is known."

After John C. Frémont, governor of the Arizona Territory, resigned, acting governor John J. Gosper swiftly moved against the lawlessness in Cochise County by appointing Wyatt Earp to drive out the outlaws. In retaliation, Sheriff Behan reopened the O.K. Corral case.

At 10:50 p.m. on Saturday, March 18, 1882, after returning from a musicale at Schieffelin Hall, Morgan Earp was ambushed. He was playing a late round of billiards at the Campbell and Hatch Billiard Parlor against owner Bob Hatch. Dan Tipton, Sherman McMaster and Wyatt watched, having received threats that same day.

The assailant shot Morgan through the upper half of a four-pane windowed door, as the bottom two window panes had been painted over. The door opened onto a dark alley that ran through the block between Allen and Fremont Streets. Morgan, who was about ten feet from the door, was struck on the right side, and the bullet shattered his spine, passed through his left side and entered the thigh of mining foreman George A.B. Berry. Another bullet lodged in the wall near the ceiling over Wyatt's head. Several men rushed into the alley but found the shooter had fled.

After Morgan was shot, his brothers tried to help him stand, but Morgan said, "Don't, I can't stand it. This is the last game of pool I'll ever play." They moved him to the floor near the card room door. Dr. William Miller arrived first, followed by Drs. Matthews and George Goodfellow. They all examined Morgan. Goodfellow, recognized in the United States as the nation's leading expert at treating abdominal gunshot wounds, concluded that Morgan's injuries were fatal.

While Wyatt and the youngest brother, Warren, were escorting Virgil and his wife to Tucson, Wyatt shot and killed Frank Stilwell, one of the Cowboys. Because he knew the conditions in Tombstone, Sheriff Paul did not issue warrants for the Earps, but Sheriff Behan deputized Curly Bill

Introduction

Old City Hall, Fremont Street, 1933. Library of Congress.

Brocius and the other gunslingers of the Cowboy faction to arrest the Earps or shoot them on sight. The county, territory and eventually the nation were subjected to the spectacle of the federal posse and the county posse stalking each other across the Arizona desert—Wyatt with federal warrants for the arrest of the Cowboys and Behan with no legal justification at all.

After Wyatt killed Curly Bill at an ambush at Iron Springs, the remaining Cowboys fled to Mexico. The surviving Earps traveled north into Colorado.

The new territorial governor, F.A. Trittle, had just taken his post when the murder of Morgan Earp escalated matters. On investigation, he sent an urgent appeal to President Chester Arthur asking for funds to set up a regional police force to deal with the situation. Arthur did one better and requested aid in a special message to both houses of Congress on April 26, 1882. Congress suggested using the army instead. On May 3, Arthur's Presidential Proclamation threatened martial law by May 15 unless the situation was rectified.

Governor Trittle and Pima County sheriff Paul told Governor Pitkin of Colorado that they could not guarantee the safety of the Earps, so Pitkin refused extradition. That was the end for the Earps. Wyatt followed the frontier wherever it went. Eventually, he retired in Los Angeles, where he died in bed in 1929. Over his long career, he was never wounded.

In July, Johnny Ringo—the last Cowboy outlaw leader—was killed near Turkey Creek. There were still plenty of criminals and dangerous

Introduction

men around, enough to make "Texas John" Slaughter's career as Cochise County sheriff famous, but the reign of terror was over. With federal interest aroused, Sheriff Behan did not run for reelection. Instead, he became the assistant warden at the Yuma Territorial Prison. He was later promoted to superintendent.

Tombstone eventually settled down to respectable prosperity. Two fires (June 22, 1881, and May 25, 1882) wiped out most of the business district, but it was promptly rebuilt. The prosperous times continued until 1883. By 1884, the price of silver had led mine owners to attempt to reduce wages from $4.00 a day to $3.50. The union struck, and violence at the mines brought what outlawry had never brought—more troops from Fort Huachuca.

In 1886, water filled the mines, and despite several attempts to pump the water out, the mines were closed. Two-thirds of the population left the town shortly afterward. Two brief periods of prosperity occurred, one in 1890 and another in 1902, but they did not last long. In 1929, the county seat was moved to Bisbee, and Tombstone lost its last reason for existing. But the town proved too tough to die. It pulled itself together, began restoration and rebuilding and found a new life as a tourist attraction. In 1961, it was declared a National Monument.

This historic landmark illustrates much of the flavor and vitality of the Wild West. As one of its historians, John Myers, wrote, "The great thing about Tombstone was not that there was silver in the veins of the adjacent hills, but that life flowed hotly and strongly in the veins of the people."

1
BIG NOSE KATE'S SALOON

On September 9, 1880, the *Arizona Daily Star* announced that Sylvester B. Comstock opened the "most elegant hostelry in Arizona," the Grand Hotel. Located on Allen Street between Fourth and Fifth Streets, the hotel was luxuriously furnished. Its rooms provided thick carpeting, and the walls were decorated with costly oil paintings. The hotel contained sixteen bedrooms fitted with solid walnut furnishings, toilet stands, fine fixtures and elaborate wallpaper. The lobby was adorned with three elegant crystal chandeliers, and the kitchen boasted hot and cold running water. An excellent description of what the hotel looked like was printed in the *Tombstone Epitaph* on September 9, 1880:

> *Through the courtesy of Mr. H.V. Sturm an* Epitaph *reporter yesterday paid a visit to and made a brief inspection of the new hotel christened the grand which will be formally open for dinner this evening at five o'clock. The general size and character of the structure have been mentioned so often during the course of construction that further mention would be superfluous and we will confine ourselves to a description of the interior appointments of it. Passing into the building by the front entrance the first thing that strikes the eye is a wide and handsome staircase covered by an elegant carpet and supporting a heavy black walnut banister. Thence upstairs to the main hall, and turning to the right, we are ushered into a perfect little bijou of costly furniture and elegant carpeting known as the bridal chamber. This room occupies half of the main front and is connected with the parlor by folding*

Big Nose Kate's Saloon sits on the location of the old Grand Hotel. *Photo by the author.*

doors through which the reporter passed, and entering the parlor was more than astonished by the luxurious appointments. A heavy Brussels carpet of the most elegant style and finish graces the floor, the walls are adorned with rare and costly oil paintings; the furniture is of walnut cushioned with the most expensive silk and rep, and nothing lacks, save the piano which will be placed in the position shortly. On down through the main corridor peeping now and then into the bedrooms, sixteen in number, each of them fitted with walnut furniture and carpeted to match: spring mattresses that would tempt even a sybarite, toilet stands and fixtures of the most approved pattern, the walls papered, and to crown all, each room having windows. All are outside rooms thus obviating the many comforts in close and ill-ventilated apartments. Returning we pass down the broad staircase and turning to the left are in the office and reading room. Here we met Mr. R.J. Pryke, the polite and affable clerk, so well known to Yosemite tourists in California. The office fixtures are as is common in first class hotels and fully in keeping with the general character of the house. The dining room adjoining next invites inspection. Here we find the same evidence of good taste in selection and arrangement that is so marked a feature of the whole interior. Three elegant chandeliers are pendant from the handsome centerpieces, walnut tables, extension, and plain, covered with cut glass, china, silver castors and the latest style of cutlery are among the many attractions of this branch of the cuisine.

Thence into the kitchen where we find the same evidence before mentioned; an elegant Montagin range 12 feet in length, with patent heater, hot and cold faucets, in fact, all the appliances necessary to feed five hundred persons at a few hours notice are present. The bar occupies the east half of the main front and is in keeping with the general furnishings. Want of space prevents more than this cursory glance at the Grand and its appliances for the comfort and convenience of guests. A Grand (no pun intended) invitation ball will take place this evening.

During its short life, the hotel housed some of Tombstone's most famous residents, including Wyatt and Virgil Earp, Doc Holliday and even members of the Clanton Gang. The hotel had a small role in the famous gunfight at the O.K. Corral. The night before the gunfight, Ike Clanton and the two McLaury brothers were registered guests. After the duel, the Earp brothers took refuge at the Grand by barricading themselves in one of its upper rooms—defying arrest by Sheriff Behan.

The name of the saloon under the Grand Hotel was identified in the *Tombstone Weekly Epitaph* on April 10, 1882:

Messrs, Alderson & Gratton will open the saloon under the Grand Hotel, formerly known as the Grotto, tomorrow evening. It is hereafter to be known as the Fountain. An elegant lunch has been prepared, and an orchestra of three pieces will be in attendance to discourse sweet music to while away the hours. A cordial invitation is extended to the public to come out and drink.

The end of the Grand Hotel came on May 25, 1882, when a fire swept from the Occidental Saloon. Once the blaze reached the wooden staircase on the outside of the Grand Hotel, the building went up in flames. Above ground, the only things that remained standing were seven great arches and floor joists. The rest of the building collapsed into the basement, where the hotel's bar was located.

Instead of rebuilding the hotel, Comstock chose to erect another structure, to be called the Grand Hotel Building. It was large enough to contain several businesses. Jakey's restaurant, card rooms and a bar occupied the ground floor. The basement was leased out to become the next incarnation of the Fountain Saloon.

In May 1942, another fire destroyed most of the building. When it was rebuilt, the adobe façade became a functional part of the structure. It then became the Allen Street Bar. In the 1970s, it was sold and became Big Nose Kate's Saloon. Some changes have been made to the original structure over the years. The bar area—originally in the basement—is now located on the main level. The basement itself is now a popular gift shop in town. Not only does the saloon continue to be popular among the locals and tourists, it is said to be the home of a couple of spectral ones as well.

The first report of paranormal activity at Big Nose Kate's Saloon occurred when the basement of the building was being renovated to create a gift shop. The original staircase to the basement was located on the outside of the structure facing Allen Street. (This area is where the dressing rooms are located today.) One evening, the owners and a few employees were sitting on the stairs in the dark enjoying a few drinks after a long day of work when they heard the sound of footsteps coming from the darkness on the other side of the room. They immediately turned on their flashlights and scanned the area, but no one was there. Thinking that it was odd but not frightened by the noises, they turned off the flashlights and continued their conversation. A few minutes later, a loud moan came from the same area, and again the flashlights were turned on, only to reveal that they were alone. This time, they decided to leave for a safer environment upstairs.

As the renovations continued, they started working in the area where the footsteps and moans seemed to have originated. There was a small separate room here, like a janitor's closet, which they had been told was once the living quarters of the janitor of the Grand Hotel, a position that was called a "swamper" in those days. As the old flooring was being removed, a tunnel was discovered beneath a wooden panel toward the center of the room. It appeared that someone had been digging down to attempt to gain access to the mine tunnels that ran underneath a large portion of Tombstone. The staff soon began calling the mysterious hole the "swamper's diggings."

It was the middle of the off-season, and business was exceptionally slow, so several nights later, the manager asked the two employees on duty if they would be interested in helping him explore the newly discovered tunnel. Both readily agreed.

Outfitted with flashlights, the trio headed down to the basement and descended into the tunnel. The tunnel itself was not very large, but they managed to explore far enough to discover that it connected to one of the

The swamper's lair in the basement of the saloon. The tunnel he supposedly dug is in the lower center of the photo. *Photo by the author.*

Toughnut mine shafts. Out of fear of becoming lost, they turned back around and made their way back to the basement. As the last of the group started up into the swamper's room, a loud moan of distress echoed down the basement stairs. The group paused as the sound of hurried footsteps came thundering down the stairs.

"Someone is in the building," whispered one of the employees.

"Can't be," said the owner. "I locked the doors."

The group quickly searched the basement, but no one was there. They then ran upstairs and began a systematic search of the bar and the adjoining rooms. They were all empty, and the doors were still locked. The legend of the swamper was born.

The legend itself is mostly based on speculation. It was evident that someone had tunneled into the mine at some point in the past. If this person was indeed stealing silver from the mine, he would have had trouble selling it locally, so it must still be hidden in the basement somewhere.

One variant of the legend is that some of the miners discovered that the janitor was stealing silver from the mine. They pushed him down the stairs, and he died from the injuries sustained during the fall. It is surmised that the swamper is afraid of someone finding his hoard of silver and he is determined to protect it. Thus the reason for all of the paranormal activity.

Despite this, the renovations continued. The next major step was to dig out a portion of the wall to create an opening to the bar above. This new entrance would be fitted with a spiral staircase that would allow easy access to the gift shop below.

Bartender Michael House was one of the employees who assisted with the digging project. In many ways, it almost resembled an archaeological dig, as they discovered a variety of artifacts, mostly old bottles, as they dug out the new stairwell. For the visitor today, all of the artifacts they recovered were placed in the Swamper's Lair exhibit in the basement. One day, Michael was climbing up the stairwell on a rope when the rope mysteriously gave way. He fell to the concrete below, and after he was able to move, he discovered that the knot that he tied to the post above was still secure. How did the rope unfasten itself if the knot was still tied? Michael also said that he has been alone in the building at 3:00 a.m. and heard people run across the floor. He would check the saloon, but nobody was there.

The bottles on the wall were recovered from the spoils of digging out the spiral stairs in the center of the building. *Photo by the author.*

Haunted Tombstone

The other set of stairs leading down to the basement. Waitresses have claimed to be pushed when they reach the last stair. *Photo by the author.*

The construction of the stairwell appeared to have some effect on the odd phenomenon that was occurring, and strange things were beginning to happen upstairs as well.

Michael also spoke of an incident where a waitress at the saloon was walking across the floor and suddenly jolted as if an unseen hand had pinched her. She was in the center of the room. There was no one near her when this happened. Another unusual phenomenon that staff have reported is that drinks will levitate off the serving tray, hitting them in the chest or in the face.

The staff quickly created a nickname for the ghost, Felix.

Other witnesses have claimed to have heard disembodied voices singing and talking in empty rooms. Objects fall to the floor of their own accord, doors open and close mysteriously, lights turn on and off by themselves and silverware has been known to go flying off tables.

Bartender Jerry Fowler told me of his encounter with the ghost:

> *I was working in here one night, and I was alone. I had already closed up and was counting the money at the cash register. The door was locked, and*

I was the only one in the building. Suddenly, I heard footsteps on the dance floor behind me. I turned around, and there wasn't anyone there. So I said, "Alright Mr. Ghost if you will wait until I finish counting this money, I'll get out of here and let you have this place." Now I'm not saying that I believe in ghosts now, but I heard the footsteps and I was the only one in the building. Just as plain as day, I heard footsteps.

Another incident I heard of involved another bartender that worked here. He was the only person in the saloon and was walking to the doors to lock them up. One his way to the doors, he noticed a cowboy wearing a duster that was leaning against the bar. He said, "You are going to have to leave, I'm closing up." However, when he got to the door, he realized that he was the only one in there. He turned back to look, and no one was there. He ran across the street and called the manager, telling him, "You can go lock up Big Nose Kate's. I'm not going back over there." He hasn't been back since.

During an investigation in 1998, I talked to manager Tim Ferrick, who went by the nickname "Whiskers." His brother had worked at the saloon, and after his death, Tim and his wife moved to Tombstone. He applied for the manager position at Big Nose Kate's and was called for an interview later that evening. This was when he had his first experience with the ghost of the saloon.

The job interview was after closing time, so the manager closed and locked the doors. Tim was accompanied by his wife, Marcy. They sat with the owner in a corner table of the saloon and quickly got down to talking about the job and the saloon itself. After the interview was over, the conversation turned to the unusual paranormal occurrences that have plagued the saloon over time. Tim was aware of the ghost and a few of the stories, as his brother had mentioned them in the past.

The owner was talking about the mine shaft when suddenly he was interrupted by a loud scraping noise. One of the prominent decorative features of Big Nose Kate's saloon at that time was a balcony at the back of the main room. On top of the balcony are two mannequins, a man and a woman that are dressed in authentic 1800s period clothing. The noise appeared to be coming from that balcony. The group looked up to see the female mannequin slowly moving forward. Then, as they all watched in disbelief, the mannequin hit the railing of the balcony and flipped over it, crashing to the floor with a loud bang. They sat in stunned silence for a moment until Tim looked back up and saw the male mannequin starting to move. He yelled to the others at the table, "Hey, look at the other

Photograph taken during a ghost hunt with 94 Rock in 2009. *Author's collection.*

mannequin!" They watched as the mannequin's head turned toward the left, where the female figure had been. The trio decided to call it a night and swiftly exited the building. This incident was enough to convince both Tim and Marcy that the building was indeed haunted.

Debbie Valdez reported another ghostly experience that occurred on the balcony. One afternoon, while tending the bar, she looked up at the balcony and saw a woman dressed in a dark dress that appeared to be from the 1880s. The unidentified woman was holding a parasol and seemed to be observing the people down below. Debbie claimed that the woman was breathtaking, so much so that she had a hard time taking her eyes off of her. The mysterious woman was visible for a few minutes, and then she just vanished into thin air.

So why are there so many reports of different apparitions, and why are they wearing dark clothing? Perhaps an answer can be found in Tombstone's history. The location where the saloon sits today was once occupied by an undertaker's business. The *Tombstone Weekly Epitaph* ran a short story about it on August 20, 1887:

Undertaking rooms, as a general thing, are not cheerful places, but when elegantly fitted up as are those of A.J. Ritter in the Grand Hotel Building, on Allen Street, they go far towards removing the gloomy surroundings. The office, which occupies the entire front of the large room has been carpeted with rich body Brussels, while the furniture is correspondingly elegant. A portiere hung with heavy drapery separates this parlor-like apartment from the stockroom where a large and varied assortment of burial caskets is to be found. Still further to the rear are two other large rooms, one of which is used as a storeroom and the other as a morgue. Everything about the place is as neat as wax, and taken altogether it is undoubtedly the most complete establishment of the kind in the southwest.

There are two types of ghostly phenomena that appear to occur the most. The first is the sound of someone wearing heavy boots walking up and down the stairs. The mysterious footsteps have been heard walking across the dance floor. This particular phenomenon is often very annoying to the managers and employees at the saloon. Tim recalled that this would frequently happen after closing. Sometimes after hearing the footsteps, he would rush to the stairs in the hope of catching the person making the sounds. However, as soon as he reached the stairs, the noises would abruptly stop and the adjoining rooms would be empty. After the saloon installed a security system, he caught the sounds of the disembodied footsteps on the audio of the video. Again, the rooms were empty, and the motion detection of the surveillance system did not activate.

The second common type of ghostly activity involves the staff, particularly the waitresses. Unseen hands pinch or slap them on the behind, poke them, pull their hair and grab their shoulders. In 2009, during a joint investigation with Tombstone Paranormal, manager Misty said that it happened to her fairly frequently since she started working there.

The freakiest thing that Misty has seen at the saloon occurred one evening when she and a co-worker were putting the chairs up on the tables after closing. The bullhorns that hung on the wall behind the stage suddenly flew off the wall and traveled twenty feet across the dance floor before hitting a table. While no one was injured, the experience was quite startling.

In Search of the Swamper

The legend of the swamper seems to be built more on speculation than fact. If you begin to ponder the elements of the legend, you end up with more questions than you do answers.

The first would be is the shaft in the basement actually connected to any of the mines below? Even during my first visit to the saloon in 1986, the shaft was filled in. Articles that I have read in the local newspapers have stated that if one stood upon the roof of the Grand Hotel, you could practically see down the shafts of several mines. The effort in such a task would have been quite excessive, but it could be plausible.

Another justifiable question would be how it was known that the tunnel in the saloon's basement was dug during the 1800s. During my research, I was unable to locate anything that indicated the existence of the tunnel before the legend of the swamper existed. It could have been created just as easily in the 1940s or any other date for that matter. If someone was getting into the mine, they would be bringing up silver ore, which would still have to be processed to extract the silver. Was that done? If so, where was that done?

I also researched the brief period of time in which the Grand Hotel existed to identify any deaths or acts of violence that might shed some light on the swamper's story. I was able to find only two deaths that actually occurred inside the hotel. The first was Archie McBride, the hotel's manager, who passed away on May 19, 1882. His funeral was held inside the hotel. The second death was that of Charles Carter, who died from an unidentified sickness in the hotel on January 22, 1882.

As for acts of violence, I located only one. It happened in February 1882, when a pistol shot was heard in front of the hotel. When the crowd went for the spot where the shot was heard, they discovered that a carelessly handled gun went off, shooting its owner in the knee. So the element that the swamper was murdered by miners does not hold much credibility.

However, before you start thinking that I am trying to debunk all of the paranormal activity that has been reported at the saloon for the past forty years, there is one more story I have to tell.

During my first formal investigation at Big Nose Kate's Saloon, I witnessed something firsthand. I was talking to one of the bartenders while he was cleaning up after the bar had closed. We were just chit-chatting, not about ghosts or anything. I was interested in what it was like to live in the town of Tombstone, and he was more than happy to oblige me. My fellow

The Toughnut mine. *Library of Congress.*

investigator Ash Thompson had just packed up the little bit of equipment that we had brought and was taking it back to the car.

While we were talking, we heard a strange sound coming from the opposite end of the bar. It had a slight ring to it as if something made out of glass was moving. We both looked in the direction of the noise to see a beer mug levitate off the bar. It hung, suspended in the air about a foot above the bar, for a fraction of a second. Suddenly, it was launched away from the bar, traveling across the saloon, where it eventually landed with a crash. I was stunned and, for once, at a lack of words. The bartender, however, acted casual as he pulled a slip of paper out from underneath the bar. I asked him what he was doing, and he replied, "We have to keep track of the ones that get broken by the ghosts." Apparently, this was something that happened fairly regularly.

I was able to search the area of the bar where the beer mug had been. There were no springs, secret hatches, magnets or any other such device that could have made that mug do what it did.

Before this event, I was extremely skeptical of the existence of ghosts and the paranormal. My interest was more in solving mysteries than it was trying to prove that paranormal things actually happen. However, after witnessing something firsthand, I began to accept that unusual things do happen and that they are worth investigating and researching.

My co-investigator Ash never lets me live down what happened at the saloon on that hot summer night. Even when I successfully debunked another haunting by finding an alternative explanation, he quickly reminded me of the incident that happened at Big Nose Kate's. Swamper or not, there really is something quite unusual going on there.

2
THE BIRD CAGE THEATRE

The Bird Cage Theatre was opened on December 26, 1881, by proprietor William J. "Billy" Hutchinson. He was the former manager of the E. Fontana dancehall next door at Allen and Sixth Streets. The Bird Cage kept its doors open twenty-four hours a day, seven days a week. Business at the Bird Cage thrived, and the theater/saloon operated around the clock. It featured a multitude of attractive dancing girls who doubled as barmaids and prostitutes between the shows and during intermissions. The stage shows at the Bird Cage started at nine o'clock in the evening and typically lasted about four hours. The beer was fifty cents if it was purchased on the main floor, but the price doubled if it was bought from one of the private curtained boxes upstairs.

Soon the saloon/theater combo not only gained a reputation as the rowdiest entertainment place in Tombstone, it was reputed to be the wickedest theater between New Orleans and San Francisco as well. The Bird Cage also hosted masquerade balls featuring cross-dressing entertainers performing strange antics and singing raunchy ballads in the most outrageous female costumes.

The design of the theater was similar to many other entertainment establishments that existed throughout the West. Just inside the main entrance was a large wooden bar that catered to the thirst of the audience. After the patrons picked up their drinks, they entered the main hall of the theater. The entertainment was conducted on a stage about five feet above the main floor and fifteen feet square. The stage itself was lit by a row of gas jets that ran along the front side. The evening's entertainment typically started with a variety show. After the performance was over, the wooden benches were moved off to the side and stacked up so the audience could dance and drink until dawn.

Behind the stage at the Bird Cage is a set of stairs that lead to the lower level. It is 80 percent the size of the building's upper floor, and these rooms reveal an untouched site from over one hundred years ago. The main room of this level consists of a sizeable private poker room with a small bar and fixtures. This room accommodated the private high-rollers' poker game. The game seated seven players and a house dealer.

The minimum buy-in was $1,000. The game played around the clock for eight years, five months and three days. Some of America's most famous businessmen, such as Adolphus Busch and George Randolph Hearst, played alongside Diamond Jim Brady, Bat Masterson, Dick Clark, Doc Holliday and a host of other famous gamblers of the Wild West.

Over that eight-year period, $10 million exchanged hands, and the house took 10 percent. At the far end of the poker room, an old iron gate opens into the liquor and wine room, which still retains its wine and whiskey casts. The downstairs bordello rooms reveal the unspoken visions of the ladies of the night and their clientele. The ruffled-up beds and scattered clothes are real. The original faded carpets and drapes and unique furniture are complemented by the different articles of a former brothel. According to

The Bird Cage Theatre, 1935. *Library of Congress.*

One of the private rooms downstairs that was also used for prostitution. *Photo by the author.*

local lore, the end room is where Wyatt Earp and Josephine Sarah Marcus carried on their illicit love affair while she was working at the Bird Cage.

The one design feature that made the Bird Cage unique was its bird cages. These were fourteen private boxes, seven on each side of the main hall, erected high up on the walls. Patrons entered the boxes by ascending a narrow stairway near the front door and following hallways that ran the length of the building behind the boxes. The boxes had a specific purpose, as the waitresses could entertain in private once they had successfully solicited a customer from downstairs. Heavy red-velvet drapes could be drawn to ensure privacy. The cost of renting a box for the evening was twenty-five dollars.

A glimpse into what the Bird Cage was like can be found in the *Arizona Daily Star* newspaper. A correspondent from the paper visited the theater and wrote about his experience on October 19, 1882:

> From its name, anyone would be led to believe it was the abode of canaries, but to the contrary, it is the "cats" retreat. I have heard of the cats capturing the canary, but these cats capture bald heads and guileless youth. The other

evening, deeming it my beholden duty, as a Star *special correspondent, I visited this noted place of amusement which is situated on Allen Street, between Fifth and Sixth. After depositing two-bits with the doorkeeper, I entered a hall filled with old age, middle age, bald head age (next to stage) youthful age and boy age all sitting around tables drinking promiscuously with the "cats." I seated myself at one of them and was surveying the gallery when a dizzy dame came along and seated herself alongside me and playfully threw her arms around my neck and coaxingly desired me to "set 'em up." All knowing my bashful and guileless ways can imagine my "set back." I thought that all of the congregated audience had their eyes on me, and the hot blood surged through my cheeks. Her bosom was so painfully close to my cheek that I believed I had again returned to my infantile period. To escape from this predicament, I immediately ordered them up. She and I, after drinking the liquid, parted at last—she* [to] *search for some other gullible "gummie." During the evening a like operation occurred with me at least a dozen times, all with different "dizzies." The variety performance was very good. The only objection I entertained was the manner in which the girls dressed, being too much on the order of mother Eve while in the Garden of Eden. But it seems to please high-forehead gentlemen occupying the seats next to the stage. The Bird Cage is run nearly on the same style as Buckley's in San Francisco, and is a paying institution. Great improvements are being made this week. A larger stage is being built. Some of the talent that graced the proscenium here has left for Tucson, under engagement to Levin. I will wager that in one month from date all the bloods of your city will be broke. Variety theaters are great institutions for Proprietors, but a bad thing for youth, for it keeps them all broke.*

In 1932, historian Bernard Sobel recorded interviews with several burlesque stars, including Annie Ashely, who performed at the Bird Cage in 1882. The Bird Cage, which opened just two months after the gunfight at the O.K. Corral, was caught up in the feud between the Earps and the Cowboys. In Annie's words:

Earning money was then exciting, to say the least. Every night the feudists would come to the theatre; sometimes meet each other, and shoot it out then and there. The boxes were built in a ring like a horseshoe, and one gang would sit on one side and the other opposite. Once our blackface comedian, Billy Hart, was on the stage when a cowboy came in and shot the wig off his head, just for devilment.

> *As soon as trouble started everyone used to drop down and lie flat on his face. Everybody. If we were dancing, and the shooting commenced, the lights would go out, and we'd lie down flat on our stomachs for protection.*
>
> *As fickle as the barometer was the change in conditions. One morning the feud would be on, then a dead quiet intended to deceive the enemy. Suddenly another feud was on. It was between the famous Earp brothers, who were the marshals, Curly Bill, a Mexican, and Frank Stillwell, a nice quiet man, though an outlaw. One night something serious happened. Morgan Earp was killed while in the Green Chop House by a shot which came in through the window while he was playing billiards. That renewed the battle. For a few hours everything was quiet. An ominous quiet, a silence intended to cheat the enemy into believing that everything was alright again. But the Earp brothers were out to avenge Morgan's death and the next day sixteen men lay strewn on the sidewalk, sprawled out in their own blood. Dead. Everyone could see them lying right there. Then they got and killed Frank Stillwell and Curly Bill out on a prairie somewhere between Tombstone and Dunning.*

While some of Annie's recollections may be sort of a tall tale, many of the elements she conveyed about working at the Bird Cage resonate with similar accounts.

According to legend, Doc Holliday occasionally dealt faro games at the Bird Cage. One night, Johnny Ringo, who hated Doc with a passion, was passing Doc's table. When Holliday slurred, "Care to buck the tiger, Johnny? It's the gustiest game in town." Ringo wheeled around. He removed his bandana and said to Holliday, "Care to grab to the other end of this bandanna? This is the deadliest game in town!"

Doc Holliday stood and smiled. "Sure Johnny, I'm your huckleberry, and this may be my lucky day."

In this type of duel, two men grab opposite ends of a bandanna and fire at each other, at point-blank range, generally killing both participants. Ringo also was intoxicated, but fortunately, Curly Bill grabbed Ringo's arm at the last second and moved him out of the way. Curly Bill yelled, "Hell Doc! He's drunk!" as both men fired and missed. Holliday, also in a drunken stupor, answered, "Broncos, I drink more by 10:00 a.m. than he can all day." Holliday then walked off. This handkerchief duel took place in the Bird Cage Theatre, between the faro table and the orchestra pit.

The Bird Cage has many other legends, and one of the most famous is a deadly fight between two soiled doves in 1882. It involved a prostitute called Gold Dollar. She was first known as Little Gertie, but with her petite frame, long golden-blonde hair and rate of a gold dollar as payment for her services, she took on the business name of Gold Dollar. She plied her trade at the Crystal Palace, which was located a block away from the Bird Cage Theatre. Although she was tiny in stature, she was feisty and known to have a mean streak.

Gold Dollar also had a live-in lover, a high-stakes gambler named Billy Milgreen, and she was said to have been very possessive of him and threatened any woman who touched or flirted with him. For the most part, the women of the town were afraid of the petite prostitute and stayed away from Billy.

Eventually, trouble came to town in the form of an attractive prostitute named Margarita. With her creamy bronze skin, this sensual, mysterious woman took a job at the Bird Cage Theatre.

Even though Margarita was aware of Gold Dollar and Billy's relationship, it didn't stop her from flirting with him. Gold Dollar threatened to cut out Margarita's heart if she didn't back off. Billy, knowing what Gold Dollar was capable of, promised her that he would have nothing to do with the newest employee of the Bird Cage.

One evening, Billy received news that a high-stakes poker game was going to be held at the Bird Cage, and he wanted in. Gold Dollar was working at the Crystal Palace that night and made him promise to stay away from Margarita. Excited about playing the game, he wholeheartedly agreed and ran off to the Bird Cage in the hopes of getting rich.

Some stories say that Gold Dollar didn't trust Billy to begin with and she went down to the Bird Cage to check things out for herself. Other accounts suggest that someone told her that Margarita was flirting with her man, and she ran down the street to the Bird Cage in a fit of rage. Regardless, she arrived just in time to see Margarita sitting in the gambler's lap.

She busted through the doors and rushed over to where they were sitting. She grabbed a fistful of Margarita's hair and pulled her off Billy. Margarita tried to fight back against the angry woman, but she was no match for her enraged temper. Gold Dollar pulled out a four-inch stiletto from her garter and stabbed the other woman in the side. Margarita, mortally wounded, died before a doctor could reach her.

When the sheriff was called, Gold Dollar ran out of the Bird Cage and hid the stiletto outside the building. Margarita's body was taken away, the blood was cleaned up and the Bird Cage roared on.

No murder charges were brought against Gold Dollar because the murder weapon was never found. The legend says that several months later, Billy

Milgreen quietly left Tombstone and was never heard from again. Perhaps he and Gold Dollar got together in some other rip-roaring mining town, their bond sealed in blood, but it's possible their paths never crossed again.

Surprisingly, a stiletto was found in the 1980s when the privy behind the theater was dug out during construction.

In 1883, Hutchinson sold the Bird Cage to Hugh McCrum and John Stroufe. For the next three years, they put on several variety shows and kept the theater open.

In 1886, Joe Bignon, a variety entrepreneur, bought the theater. He redecorated the building, installed new seats and used his connections in the entertainment business to hire a diverse group of performers. He also renamed it, calling the new enterprise the Elite Theater. He hired magicians, ventriloquists, trapeze acts, high-kicking dancers, even a troop specializing in the circus feat of human pyramids. Joe's wife was called Big Minnie. A local writer described her as "six feet and 230 pounds of loveliness in pink tights." Minnie sang, played piano and did ballet skits for the audience. On more than one occasion, she also acted as the theater's bouncer. A reporter from the *Prospector* wrote a brief piece for the newspaper that enumerated Minnie's extra duties:

> *On May 11, 1889, an intoxicated woodchopper from the Dragoon mountains brandished a pistol when bartender Charley Keen ask him for an additional nickel for his next shot of Mumm's Extra Dry. Charley looked at the man, and he had his eyes fixed on Charley. At this moment, Mrs. Bignon entered, and Charley asked her to stay there while he went after the sheriff, Bob Hatch, to put the man out. She answered that she would put him out herself, and proceeded to put the objectionable visitor out the front door. However, on the way to jail, he broke free from his captors and began exchanging shots with the officers outside of the Bird Cage. He was quickly subdued a second time and finally incarcerated.*

In 1888, travelers to Tombstone reported that the Bird Cage was one of the liveliest attractions they had seen anywhere, and between the hours of 8:00 p.m. and 5:00 a.m., it lived up to its reputation. The place continued to offer the same sensual delights as it did during Billy Hutchinson's management. It was still almost entirely patronized by men looking for women, gambling and various other entertainment. But under Bignon, the Bird Cage seemed to reach a more feverish frenzy. Sometimes the riotous entertainment erupted almost beyond Bignon's control. Starved for diversion and clouded

In 1933, the theater did not have a boardwalk. *Library of Congress.*

by alcohol, the clientele was always on edge. Amid the noise, delirium and nearly nude ladies, passions rose and tempers flared as shots from pistols zipped around the place. Sometimes the fighting would spill out onto the streets in front of the theater. These incidents occasionally made their way into the local paper, often with complaints from the town's residents: "A disgraceful row between an attorney of this city and a soiled dove occurred at the Bird Cage last evening. Officers flopped the row but did not arrest the offenders. This is not the first time this kind of a disgraceful row has occurred, and our officers should do their duty."

One of the more unusual acts at the Bird Cage in 1889 was called the human fly. In this performance, women, dressed in theatrical tights and scanty costumes, walked upside down on the ceiling over the stage. It was not an illusion—they actually were suspended above the stage. This type of act gained some notoriety in theaters around the West for a short while. The trick was that their shoes had special clamps on them that fit into holes bored into the ceiling to support them. Unfortunately, one of the performers was killed when one of the clamps slipped and she fell.

Carmelita Gimenes, a well-known singer at the Bird Cage, was living with Frederick Baker, a young actor who had also taken a job at the Bird Cage. The couple was living in an abode adjoining the theater when things began to go sour. During the coroner's inquest on August 17, 1888, Baker recalled:

> *All I know, I have been living with her for four or five months. A few nights ago after we got through work at the Bird Cage Theatre, where we are both employed, after the show we came home. After we had retired for the night, she commenced a crying. I asked her the cause of it. She answered it was not concerning me what she was crying about. I asked her if it was about me and she said no, it was something else. I have noticed of late that she was not in her right spirits, rather downhearted and melancholy therefore I did not trouble her no farther [sic] or ask her any questions. I was in the kitchen at the time she took the poison. After rehearsal yesterday I saw her vomit alongside the washstand. I asked her what was the matter with her and asked what was the cause of it. She said she took some medicine to make her sick. I asked what it was and she would not tell me. I thought it was an emetic. I went up town and came back again. It was about 5 o'clock p.m. As I came in I saw an old lady sitting there talking to her, and I saw she was sick and therefore I went in the kitchen. Carmelita followed me in and asked me what I was going to do, and I told her I was going to cook supper, and she said No! I will cook it myself, and I answered No! You are*

sick, you lay down, and I will cook supper. She said will you cook supper for me too and I said yes. With that, she throwed her arms around my neck and kissed me and then she went into the other room and laid down. I not thinking there was anything the matter with her, started in to cook supper. I did not know nothing more until the children came and then her sister. I did not pay any attention to them at all as they come there pretty near every day. The next thing I know Josephine, her niece, asked me if I knew what was the matter with Carmelita. I said she's only a little sick. She said No! She has poisoned herself, go and get a doctor. I went out and found Doctor Willis and brought him to her. He asked me on the way what she had poisoned herself with. I told him I did not know. He said, well how do you know she poisoned herself? I said, her sister told me. That is about all she would tell me what she did use to poison herself.

Dr. Willis gave Carmelita an emetic and discovered that she had taken two teaspoons of Rough on Rats, an arsenic poison. He administered several antidotes to no avail, and Carmelita died at five o'clock the following morning. A short time later, the paper noted that the Elite had closed for the night out of respect for Carmelita, who had finally succeeded in ending her own life.

The bar and office door, 1945. The entrance for the theater was on the opposite side of the room. *Author's collection.*

For the girls of the Bird Cage, the irony of their lives could not have been sharper. Inside the theater, they tantalized and teased, achieving a degree of power and control. Most of them liked to believe that the entertainment aspect of their job was their real profession. But for many, it was not. And outside, they were shunned and alone, broke and sick. But at least the women of the Bird Cage managed to escape the desolation of the cribs on Sixth Street.

Like so many other mining towns, Tombstone eventually began to decline during the early 1890s. Bignon sold the building and closed its doors in the summer of 1892. He also shipped the props and some furnishings to Albuquerque for storage. He eventually returned to Tombstone and, for a time, ran variety performances at the Crystal Palace Saloon, recruiting a few of the Bird Cage old-timers such as singer Ella Ward and comic Jessie Reed. He made a go of it for about two years before he finally gave up and closed it for good in 1899.

The old theater changed hands again in 1900 when it was purchased by Charles L. Cummings, the mayor of Tombstone. He wanted to use the building for storage for all of his treasures that he'd collected in Cochise County.

In 1929, Tombstone held its first Helldorado celebration. The floors of the old theater were cleaned and repaired, and for a short time, it was reopened for the public. When Charles passed away in 1930, his widow, Margaret, was determined to carry out his dream to have his treasures publicly displayed inside the Bird Cage. However, by 1931, the theater was beginning to show its age. The *San Bernardino County Sun* published an article on September 18 of that year describing a rather unfortunate accident:

> *The Bird Cage Theatre, where world celebrities entertained when Tombstone was one of the "live spots" in the West during the early mining days, was in wreckage today. An adobe wall crashed down, causing the old theater to crumble in several places.*
>
> *When the Bird Cage was flourishing Tombstone had a population of 15,000, compared to approximately 500 at present. Residents said the damage will be repaired if possible.*

Finally, in 1934, she finished the renovations of the building. The front section was leased out as a coffee shop. In 1946, Margaret sold the theater to Harry and Minnie Ohm, who added restrooms to the building in 1947. Their primary effort was not to restore the theater but to keep it the best

The theater in 1935. The entry can be seen on the left with the tapestry of Fatima in the center. *Author's collection.*

preserved original building in Tombstone. After Minnie's death in 1967, the building passed on to William Hunley.

According to local lore, the first incidents of ghostly activity at the old Bird Cage started in 1921 when the high school was built across the street. As a result, the children who were walking to school began to say that they heard laughter and music coming from the inside of the old building. In fact, many of them were afraid to walk near it.

For the most part, tourists and employees of the Bird Cage report pleasant encounters with the paranormal. However, there was one experience that the owner would like to forget. In the 1980s, owner William Hunley was attending a séance at the Bird Cage. A prominent medium was brought in to assist in contacting the spirits that supposedly inhabited the theater. During this séance, somebody started strangling him, and everybody at the table witnessed it. The commotion caused the medium to break her trance, and finally, the violent act ceased. William had bruises on his neck for six weeks afterward.

William's son, Bill, has many stories about things suddenly materializing and disappearing. Once, a valuable antique poker chip that had been missing from a gaming table for years inexplicably reappeared in its former place. After finding the chip, Bill Hunley locked it away in a bank vault for safekeeping while he waited for a group of western scholars to authenticate it. When the scholars arrived, Hunley was alarmed to discover the chip had disappeared once again. He frantically searched for it, but the poker chip was nowhere to be found. Later, after the disappointed scholars had left, the poker chip materialized again—this time in a locked drawer of the desk in the Bird Cage Theatre.

Another unusual series of incidents involved a statue of Wyatt Earp that had been placed in one of the cribs that overlook the main room of the Bird Cage. The cribs are sealed off so that no one can disturb the artifacts displayed inside. Over a period of about six months, Earp's hat was consistently knocked off and thrown out into the middle of the floor below, a distance of about fifteen feet. At one point the statue of Earp was turned completely around so that his face was pointed toward the wall. Confident that the mischief was not being caused by the living, the management was quite baffled by what was going on. Then, Hunley was informed by a local historian that the crib in which Earp's statue was located was actually the crib that was often rented by the Clantons when they came to the Bird Cage.

The worn steps leading up to the stage. *Photo by the author.*

Billy Clanton, a rival of the Earp brothers, was shot and killed near the O.K. Corral, just down the street from the Bird Cage. After learning this, Hunley had the statue moved to the crib Earp frequented while he was alive. After this, the unusual activity stopped.

The employees of the Bird Cage Theatre have reported a multitude of unusual or bizarre happenings over the years. Quite frequently, the smell of cigar smoke will travel through the building when no one has been smoking. Many people, including tourists, have claimed to have heard the faint sounds of a woman singing to vintage music. There have been many reports of a phantom stagehand who walks across the stage wearing a visor and carrying a clipboard. Many believe that this specter is a former owner or perhaps a stagehand who has chosen to stay.

Many of the employees admit they are afraid to be alone in the theater after sunset because of the extreme amount of ghostly activity. One employee reported that after the Bird Cage had closed for the evening, he turned off the central sound system for the building. He and another employee went down into the basement and went inside one of the bordello rooms, the same place where Wyatt Earp supposedly had an affair with a courtesan named Josephine Marcus. Soon they both heard an unintelligible voice coming out of the sound system, which then began blaring the song "Red River Valley." The two frightened employees were the only living people inside the building that night. One of them stated later: "You never want to be in here after nine o'clock at night—that's when stuff really starts happening."

Employee Bill Clanton, a descendant of O.K. Corral victim Billy Clanton, said he often heard things he couldn't explain coming from the old opera house and gambling hall, now a dusty museum. "They're always moving around in there," Clanton said, pointing to the museum. "There's laughing and carrying on you can't explain. You can smell smoke around the dice table. I tell them, 'You leave me alone, and I'll leave you alone.'"

Sarah Washburn, a sales clerk in the Bird Cage gift shop, said she had a frightening experience her second day on the job. Washburn, whose work uniform is a dancehall costume, a low-cut taffeta and lace dress with red feathers in her hair, walked through the museum and seemed to catch the attention of one of the theater's spirits.

"'I'll be right down,' he said to me. He was walking up the stairs to the second floor." She remembered he smelled like cigar smoke. She made some inquiries and found there was no one in the museum at the time.

"I think he wanted to buy me," she said. "Oh yeah, I believe in ghosts."

The view from the stage today. The entry to the theater is now on the right. *Photo by the author.*

Another docent of the Bird Cage, Nova Fleury, described her first sighting of an apparition in the theater.

> *I saw an apparition of a young woman who opened the curtain; she was between the ages of eighteen and twenty. She was leaning on the balustrade, and when she looked at the balustrade, she seemed to say that the place was unoccupied and there was no one in the alcoves. She was only wearing a bloomer, so she stood out.*

Another reoccurring apparition is that of a woman wearing a white dress and a bonnet. She has been seen on the security cameras in the poker room in the basement when no one was in that place at that time. Ruth Larrison, another employee of the theater, described seeing her:

> *When I went to lock the back doors, I heard a woman, but there was no one. My co-workers were in the office and called to me, as they too had seen this woman on the security monitor. Everyone saw her go downstairs or go down*

the stairs and go through the door. Then, as we watched, we all saw her again. At first, I thought it was a real person because I did not see through it, she looked like a living person. I cannot say whether she was walking or floating because it was too stealthy. I could see the side of her face.

Another worker at the old theater had this to say about this particular apparition:

Almost everyone who works here has had an experience of some kind with the "Lady in White." I have seen her. She came down the stairwell and into the poker room. She wore a white dress and a white bonnet. She stood in front of me for a very long time without reacting to my presence at all—it's like she didn't even know I was there. She's what they call a "residual haunt." No one has ever identified who she is. A bonnet indicates she was a proper lady, and no proper ladies ever came in here. Most of us who work here think she came in with the hearse and is now trapped here.

Dean Dougherty also saw the woman in a white dress in broad daylight. He admitted that he was skeptical the first time he came into the Bird Cage. After the theater had closed, he noticed a woman in a white dress through the window, coming out of the door that leads to the main room. He came back inside and walked to the counter and told her that she should not stay here. The woman then vanished right before his eyes. There is a photograph of a woman in a white dress that goes down the stairs. We think it is the same woman.

The photograph that Dean is speaking of was taken by Donovan's Ghost Patrol in 2006. This picture was taken from the bottom of the poker room stairs in the back of the theater. Many people claim to see a female figure that has one foot stepping down. She also appears to be holding her dress up as she descends the stairs. If you look carefully off to the side, you'll see one of the Ghost Patrol's producers crouched over in the corner. Her name is Michelle, and right before the picture was taken, she yelled that she felt something run by her. Three photographs were taken in sequence, about two seconds apart, and this was photo number two. The third picture was completely normal—nothing unusual was in it. It's been featured on several of the paranormal and ghost shows, and they keep it in the lobby at the Bird Cage Theatre.

This may also be the ghost that Grant and Jason saw when their show *Ghost Hunters* visited the theater a few months afterward. Both of the

Above: The photo of the Lady in White taken by the Ghost Patrol with Donovan. *Author's collection.*

Left: Josh Hawley and the author setting up instrumentation on the stairs leading down to the poker room. *Author's collection.*

investigators described seeing a woman, about five feet tall, in a white dress wearing a bonnet. Based on the description of the apparition and the areas where the sightings occur, Carmelita Gimenes is a strong candidate for this specter. This same apparition is responsible for one of the strangest encounters that I have experienced in my thirty-plus years of paranormal investigation.

In 1998, I went to the Bird Cage with another member of the Southwest Ghost Hunters named Tiffany. However, I was not exactly looking for ghosts on this trip. I had recently become interested in using JavaScript and Flash to stitch images together to create a three-dimensional virtual environment on webpages. I really wanted to try this technique at the Bird Cage, so we arrived early to beat the crowd. The JavaScript technique required a considerable number of photographs. Practically every inch of the theater needed to be photographed so that I could connect them together to create the virtual environment. The other challenge is that I did not want anyone in any of the photographs, only the natural environment.

This particular morning, the theater opened with two employees. One watched the front while the other went to the gift store at the rear of the building. We were the first people in that day, and I immediately started the grueling task of taking pictures, starting at the front door and making my way toward the gift shop downstairs.

One hour and several hundred photos later, I was finally on the stage. Tiffany, who had long since become quite bored with the activity, had gone downstairs to the poker room. I was just about to finish up with the last set of photographs for the backstage area when an employee came up the steps. She was a woman in her late twenties, long black hair that was tucked up under a white bonnet. She wore a white blouse that was fastened with a multitude of small white pill-type buttons and a light gray skirt. She smiled at me as I paused and waited for her to pass out of my shot. She immediately went to stage right and descended the steps to the poker room. I took the last set of shots and turned to follow her down. As I started down the stairs, I almost ran into Tiffany, who was walking up.

"Did you ever look under the stage?" she asked. "There are several old beer kegs down there. I wonder if they are the original ones that were used by the bar?"

"Well, why don't you ask the employee that just passed you?" I replied.

Tiffany suddenly had a rather strange look on her face. She explained that she had not seen anyone while she was downstairs. She was alone and merely waiting for me to catch up.

Haunted Tombstone

Old beer and whiskey kegs along with several other artifacts are located under the stage. *Photo by the author.*

Of course, this didn't make any sense. I had just seen her, and there was no way that Tiffany could have missed her. At first, I thought that she was just joking around, trying to trick me. However, she was quite adamant. The only other person that she saw downstairs was the employee who was behind the cash register in the gift shop.

So we went to the gift shop to ask the employee there if she had seen anyone else come through, since it was the only way out. After receiving yet another quizzical look, I was told that Tiffany and I were the only guests in the theater. No one had exited through the gift shop yet.

Of course, Tiffany took the missed opportunity to poke fun at me. "Cody! I can't believe you! You had a camera in your hands, and the ghost just walks right on by you!"

I thought it was just another employee. Nothing in her appearance stood out to me that would indicate that she was a ghost. It was another one of those lessons that I learned the hard way.

What's really unusual about the events taking place here is that they wildly vary in nature.

Haunted Tombstone

Teresa Benjamin told me a story about a family of tourists who had marched into the gift shop and complained that they had not seen any ghosts. Disgruntled, they left, calling the place a tourist trap.

However, when they got back home, they called Teresa to apologize. On their videotape, they discovered two frightening specters staring straight into the camera. The family talked to Teresa on the phone for half an hour describing the images. One was of a man sitting inside of the antique hearse that is on display backstage. The other was a woman in one of the bordello rooms, and she was upset at their presence. "They said it was strange," she recalled, "because they could actually see the expression on her face go from shock to rage instantly."

Perhaps the most bizarre image was one Teresa witnessed herself while watching the security monitor. In the high-stakes poker room in the basement, she saw a pair of boots and spurs walking down the hallway with absolutely no legs. The boots were walking along by themselves. She thought she just saw things, but when a couple passed through that same room moments later, they asked why that room alone was kept at such a low temperature. "They said it was so cold they couldn't stand it in there, but that room is the same temperature as the rest of the building."

The poker room downstairs under the stage. *Photo by the author.*

Haunted Tombstone

Other tourists have had ghostly encounters of their own. Here are a couple of their accounts:

While on vacation to El Paso from San Diego, I convinced the wife and son to stop by the city of Tombstone, Arizona. I had been so excited about this trip because I have wanted to visit Tombstone since I was about ten years old. We stopped by the Birdcage Theatre, which is reported to be haunted; we took the self-guided tour, and it was very creepy because it's so old. After seeing it on TV and movies, I had to experience it for myself.

Once we got to the backstage area, there were pictures along the wall of an old showgirl or prostitute who used to work there. I was standing next to my wife reading the info on the wall when she decided to walk away without telling me toward a black carriage looking thing to take photos. Just then, I felt a sharp poke on my butt, and I told her to stop playing because it hurt. She yells back at me from across the room and says "what the h*** are you talking about." When I realized I had been touched, it got absolutely frigid by the photos, and I left the room toward the front lobby. I was scared, but I did finish the tour.

You may have noticed a pattern. Although tourists often go into the Bird Cage in groups, usually only one person experiences something strange. Here is yet another such encounter:

My daughter stood at the doorway just inside the theater, and the color drained from her face. "What's the matter, Anna? You look like you've seen a ghost!"

"I only wish you were wrong, Mom," she replied. I had never seen her so distraught as she begged for us to leave.

"You can't be serious, Anna! I just paid full admission for the both of us to come in here, and this was something we both wanted to visit! Look at all this great stuff! Just think…Doc was here, Wyatt…"

"Mom, I want to go. Now!" Her face spoke of something otherworldly of which only she was aware. It took quite a bit of coercing to convince her it was just her imagination playing tricks and to just forget about it and enjoy the museum. But my efforts only took hold for a minute or two.

As she gazed up into the box seats where ladies had once entertained their paying customers, a look came over Anna's face I had never seen. In a flash, she fled the Bird Cage without hesitation and didn't look back.

The Black Mariah, Tombstone's horse-drawn hearse, now on display at the Bird Cage Theatre. *Photo by the author.*

>*I followed quickly to catch up, letting the door slam shut behind me and echo into the silent cavern where history seemed caught in a loop.* "What the heck is going on?" *I demanded to know.*
>
>"We were not alone in there, Mom."
>
>"The caretaker told me we were the first visitors this morning. But even so, it's a museum, dear. There are going to be other people arriving."
>
>"No. Not people, Mom. Ghosts."
>
>"Ghosts?"
>
>"Yes, Mom…ghosts." *The look on her face told me she was dead serious. My daughter had seen something she couldn't explain and felt the presence of the ghosts that haunt the Bird Cage.*

The *Tombstone Epitaph*, the local newspaper since 1881, has reported many ghost sightings in the area and at the Bird Cage Theatre. In a recent article, the *Epitaph* stated that the son-in-law of one of the employees of the Bird Cage became spellbound by the baby coffin that is on display in the theater's museum. He noticed that the coffin seemed to be vibrating and shot twelve rolls of film of the incident. However, when the film was developed, none of the pictures came out.

If you are looking for ghosts in Tombstone, the Bird Cage should be your first stop.

3
BRUNCKOW CABIN

On the Charleston Road between Tombstone and Sierra Vista is the site of the old Brunckow Cabin. It is set about two hundred yards off the road on a bluff overlooking the river and is known as the bloodiest cabin in all of Arizona. At least twenty-one men were killed on this site, with seventeen of those being murdered between 1858 and 1880.

Many of those unfortunate souls are buried near the cabin itself, which makes this site an unofficial graveyard. This site was owned or used by men such as Fredrick Brunckow, Ed Schieffelin, Frank Stilwell and Milton B. Duffield.

Fredrick Brunckow was a German immigrant who was born in 1830 and immigrated to the United States in 1850. He was a native of Berlin and educated at the University of Westphalia and the School of Mines at Freiberg. After coming to the United States, he worked his way west, holding a variety of jobs until he met Charles Poston of the Sonora Exploring and Mining Company. Brunckow's credentials were quite impressive, and he was soon hired. Poston was familiar with the tradition of Spanish silver mining in the San Pedro Valley, and he wanted a young, enterprising professional to prospect the area. Brunckow fit the bill and found silver in 1859. Shortly afterward, Poston sent him to New York to report his discovery and its estimated worth to the company's stockholders. Then the young German came back to Arizona and began work on his mine. Several adobe buildings, including a store, were built. Two partners, William and James Williams, were brought in, and a force of miners and laborers was recruited in Sonora.

It was a small but profitable operation. The great silver strike in the hills nine miles northeast, where Tombstone would eventually be founded, was still two decades away. If tragedy had not struck, it is very likely that Brunckow, not Ed Schieffelin, would have sparked the great days of silver mining in Cochise County. However, fate had a different plan.

On July 23, 1860, William Williams left the mine on horseback for Fort Buchanan, thirty-five miles to the southwest, to purchase a wagon load of flour. Left behind were Brunckow; James Williams, mining engineer and part-time keeper; a former schoolteacher from St. Louis named Morse; and David Brontrager, a cook.

At midnight three days later, Williams return to the mine, accompanied by the two young sons of a Sonoita rancher. The boys had the job of returning the wagon and team to the fort after the supplies were unloaded. As they approached the camp, Williams was puzzled because the sound of their arrival had not alerted any of the dogs that were kept at the camp. Suddenly, the three were stopped dead in their tracks by an ominous sign, the smell of death.

Cautiously, Williams dismounted and entered the store to investigate, using a lighted match to illuminate the area. The scene he found was one of horror. His cousin, three days dead, lay on the floor just beyond the entrance. The store itself was a wreck, looted of its merchandise. Fearful that the assassins might still be waiting in the darkness, Williams ran back to the wagon and told the boys, "Let's get back to the fort, quick, more help!" The trio rode away, not looking back until they reached Fort Buchanan. Upon their arrival, Williams told the post commander about what he had seen. The commander immediately dispatched a detail of troopers to the scene.

Later that day, the cook, Brontrager, appeared at Camp Jecker, the field headquarters of the Sonora Survey Commission. He was exhausted, bruised and bloody and almost incoherent. He said that a massacre had taken place at the mine and it was the work of the Mexican miners. The killers had all fled to Sonora, and he was the only survivor. He told the troopers that soon after Williams left for the fort, two of the miners came into the kitchen and asked for a match to light their cigars. At the same time, there were gunshots outside, and the pack of dogs began to howl. Brontrager heard shouts and cries of terror and pain. He started for the door, but the miners barred his way.

"You are a prisoner," they told him, "but we will not harm you because you are a good Catholic. We are all going to Sonora, with the goods from the store, and in time we will let you go."

Several thousand dollars' worth of merchandise that had recently arrived from St. Louis was the motive for the massacre, the cook said. As the Mexicans and their families departed with the loot piled high on the camp's seven horses and mules, Brontrager saw the victims. James Williams was shot dead in the store. Morse, who also was killed by gunfire, was lying just outside. Brunckow had been stabbed to death at the mineshaft.

"The Mexicans turned me loose just before we got to the border," Brontrager told the troopers, "and I have been wandering around here for four days."

The cook was taken to Fort Buchanan, where the commander confined him to the guardhouse as a witness should the killers be caught and to protect him from several enraged citizens, who believed that he was an ally of the murderers.

By the time the soldiers arrived at the mine, the area had become even more gruesome. There was almost nothing left of Morse and Brunckow, as wolves had eaten the majority of their corpses. The decomposition of what remained of their bodies in the hot Arizona sun was so extreme that the bodies could only be identified by the clothing they were wearing.

"It made us all sick," Sergeant Henderson later wrote in his report, "but with the help of whiskey and camphor we gave the deceased a good burial." Initially, the newspapers put the murders on the local Apaches. This would change in early August when a courier brought a message from the commandant of the Santa Cruz District in Sonora to the commander at Fort Buchanan. The message revealed that a man named Jesus Rodriguez had been captured, and under interrogation, he leaked information about the massacre at the cabin. Rodriguez was a Brunckow miner who had been boasting of the murders in Arizona in several Cananea cantinas, disposing of his share of the stolen goods in the process. The other killers, Rodriguez said, had gone to Hermosillo.

The mine was deserted from the day of the massacre until October 23, 1873, when the claim was purchased by Milton B. Duffield, the first U.S. marshal appointed to Arizona Territory. Duffield was a controversial figure, which is one way of saying that a lot of people loathed and outright hated him. However, a man named James T. Holmes also claimed to be the owner. On June 5, 1874, Duffield arrived at Brunckow's Cabin to evict Holmes from the property. As he approached, Duffield began "waving his arms and shouting like a madman." Assuming that Duffield was armed and dangerous, and aware of his violent reputation, Holmes grabbed his double-barreled shotgun. He burst out the front door, and without the slightest bit of hesitation, shot the old lawman dead. It was at this point Holmes realized that his victim was unarmed.

Duffield was accorded an obituary in the *Tucson Citizen*, which read: "He has frequently marched through the streets like an insane person, threatening violence to all who had offended him. It is claimed by some men that Duffield had redeeming qualities, but we confess we could never find them."

Duffield was buried somewhere around Brunckow Cabin, and his remains are still interred there to this day. His is just another one of several unmarked graves surrounding the cabin.

Holmes was soon arrested and tried for murder. He was found guilty and sentenced to three years in prison. However, he escaped before having a chance to serve any of his time. The local authorities did not make an effort to chase after him, and he was never seen in the Arizona Territory again.

When Ed Schieffelin, the man who founded the town of Tombstone, came into the area in 1877, he used Brunckow's Cabin as a base of operations while he prospected the rocky outcroppings to the northeast. He smelted any ore he found in the cabin's fireplace.

A few months later, Ed had worked his way over to Goose Flats, where he found the mother lode of silver and registered his claim under the name Tombstone because the U.S. Army soldiers stationed nearby had told him, "The only thing you will find out there is your tombstone."

Frank Stilwell, one of the Cowboys who was known to be involved in the murder of Morgan Earp on March 18, 1882, also had a connection with the Brunckow Cabin and mine site. Stilwell, who had been a deputy sheriff under Johnny Behan, also owned several businesses. They included several mines, a saloon, a wholesale liquor business and even a stage line.

When he met his death at the hands of Wyatt Earp in the Tucson train yards, Stilwell was the recorded owner of the Brunckow mine site and some surrounding property.

On May 20, 1897, the *Tombstone Prospector* reported that Brunckow's Cabin was the site where a gang of bandits fought over a Wells Fargo gold shipment that they had just acquired. However, the outlaws could not reach an agreement on how to divide the gold. The resulting argument led to violence, as they turned against one another and shot it out. According to the newspaper, all five of the outlaws were later found dead. The stolen gold was recovered at the scene and soon returned.

Over the next several years, many others have been found dead near the cabin. A man and his son, who were camping by the cabin one evening, were found dead several days later. A lone prospector who was exploring the mine was found near the cabin with a bullet in his back. An early settler of Tombstone told in his diary of finding a family of four massacred at the cabin, supposedly by the Apache.

In May 1897, the *Tombstone Epitaph* printed a ghost story that featured Brunckow Cabin and the haunted mine. It mentioned that every night, a menacing ghost was seen moving around the dilapidated adobe cabin. Several people attempted to investigate, but upon approaching near enough to speak, the apparition suddenly vanished, only to appear just as quickly at some other place, thus sending its pursuers on a lively and elusive chase.

The newspaper noted that some people reported hearing the sounds of mining coming from the shaft, such as "pounding on drills, pickaxes pulling away rocks, and the sawing of lumber for trusses."

This account is echoed in another newspaper story published by the *Tombstone Prospector* on May 20, 1897:

> *The halcyon days of Tombstone are often brought to memory, and even at the expense of some unfortunate. It is a pleasure to allow the mind to revert back to the 80's when this was surely the greatest mining camp on earth; when the shrill whistles of the numerous mines were deafening to the ear; when the bad man prevailed, and the music of his "gun" lulled many to sleep; when bold highwaymen plied when "life" began with the fading away of each day, and there was one continual round of pleasure. Crime then was regarded as a matter of course. Criminals held full sway, and it was a case of survival of the fittest. These reflections are brought to mind through the report of a spook which has taken possession of a long since abandoned mine. The history of which at once establish it as the appropriate habitation of ghosts. In the early days of Brunckow mine, three miles below Tombstone was the scene of much excitement; dissension arose among the owners and shooting affairs became numerous, occasionally a man was missing, and that ended it: one man was supposed to have been shot and thrown into a well, but as there were abundant men in those days an investigation was deemed needless. Five men were found at the Brunckow with their toes pointing heavenward at one time: it was an ideal rendezvous for the knight of the road. The five men found there were a party of freebooters who had raided a Wells-Fargo bullion wagon and fought over a division of the spoils. If such a thing be possible, then it is no wonder that the spirit of the departed should linger around the scene of pillage and carnage. Reputable men of Tombstone will vouch for the truthfulness of the statement that the mine is haunted. The story goes that every night can be seen*

a menacing ghost stalking around and through the dilapidated 'dobe shanty; people have attempted to investigate, but upon approaching apparently near enough to speak, the spook suddenly vanishes, only to appear as quickly at some other point, leading its would-be queriest a lively and illusive chase. There is apparently but one and when out to be seen, mining operations can be heard in the old shaft, pounding on drills, sawing lumber and working along ever and anon just as though silver had never depreciated. That there is some mysterious movements around the Brunckow is honestly believed by many here. Several of our sturdy plainsmen and mountaineers will visit this deserted mine and attempt an investigation.

In 1881, the *Arizona Democrat* also reported that "the graves lie thick around the old adobe house. Prospectors and miners avoid the spot as they would the plague, and many of them will tell you that the unquiet spirits of the departed are wont to revisit and wander about the scene."

Ever since ghost hunting has become vogue, Brunckow Cabin has been one of the top locations that ghost hunters and paranormal investigators

Donovan at the cabin ruins recording segments for the Ghost Patrol. *Photo by the author.*

want to investigate. Even the television show *Ghost Hunters* has been to this site to do an investigation.

Donovan's Ghost Patrol has been out to the site of the cabin several times. During a ghost hunt in 2017, I was able to accompany them. On this particular trip, we went to do some audio recording that would be used on future segments for Donovan's radio show. It has a unique ambiance that can be quite creepy.

While exploring the ruins, several of the investigators distinctly heard the sound of approaching footsteps. When we investigated the sounds, we found nothing. No people, no animals, just the darkness of the southern Arizonian night. The site itself can be quite dangerous, as there are several mineshafts in the area. I have been told that drug smugglers could be an issue as well. Not wanting to tempt fate, we finished the recordings and left the ghosts to their own devices.

4
The Buford House

Located on Stafford Street in Tombstone, Arizona, is the Buford House Bed and Breakfast. The Buford House was named after George Washington Buford, the original owner and builder of the adobe house constructed in 1880. The Bufords were one of Tombstone's prominent and influential families, as George was a successful mining executive. So he built the house to be one of the finest in the early history of Tombstone.

The Buford family lived in the house from 1880 until 1888. Annie Buford gave birth to several children while living in the house; unfortunately, at least three of the children died at early ages from diphtheria, whooping cough and other menacing diseases of the era.

The house has had many different owners over its long history. Sometimes, the house was used as a private residence, but it also operated as a boardinghouse or bed-and-breakfast. In the 1880s, the upstairs was one large room divided into smaller rooms by canvas walls.

Other noteworthy residents include two sheriffs, a mayor and a state senator. George and Annie Buford remained in Tombstone until 1890. Of their seven children, six were born in the home, and three died in 1886 of diphtheria. They were two, four and six years old.

We arrived at the Buford House with Polo, the producer of the Donovan show for 93.7 KRQ. After checking in, we proceeded to a variety of locations in Tombstone before returning to the bed-and-breakfast. For this ghost hunt, we were not told about the ghost story. Instead, Donovan wanted to know if we could figure out what was happening at the house by just investigating the phenomena that visitors had reported over the years.

The front of the Buford House. *Photo by the author.*

We were told that the owners believed the house was haunted by the ghost of a man who had died tragically. The owners and a multitude of guests have seen this unidentified person walking inside the home. He also has been seen on the street in front of the old adobe house.

Another common occurrence is that the doorbell rings in the middle of the night, apparently all by itself. Guests have reported hearing knocking on walls, faucets turning themselves on and off and strange lights appearing. Once in a while, women say that they have felt someone touch their hair or stroke the back of their necks when no one is around. Knocking is heard in the walls, faucets and lights go on and off by themselves and mysterious lights move across the walls of the Wicker Room. Occasionally the bed covers are pulled back, and women hear their names being called.

Another interesting story we were told concerned a sighting of a feisty old lady. One witness claimed that she saw the old lady ghost rocking on a chair in her room. She went on to say that they had an argument about whose room it was. The spirit screamed at her, "This is my room—GET OUT!" But she wouldn't budge. According to the owners, this went on all night.

With this small amount of knowledge, we started the ghost hunt. We split the team up to observe the three areas where the most paranormal activity had been reported. After several hours of observation and note-taking, the team decided to call it a night. Donovan, Jerry and Polo comprised one team, while Bob Carter and I made up the other.

The investigation itself was rather uneventful. Most of what either team encountered was quickly identified as originating from entirely explainable causes. At that time, the Southwest Ghost Hunters Association was experimenting with near-UV photography. We did manage to capture two strange photographs on the staircase. However, later analysis of the photographs created issues when we learned that there was a potential that the modifications done to the cameras may have created artifacts. At the time, the pictures created a lot of excitement, but after a full day of investigating multiple locations, we decided to call it a night.

With the ghost hunt completed, we headed off to bed. Bob asked me if he should set the alarm on the wind-up clock or not. I told him not to worry about it because the owners ring a bell in the morning to announce breakfast.

Later that night, a very interesting thing happened to Bob. He was just about to doze off when the light near the door turned off, and the lamp near the bed turned on. Bob raised up his head and said out loud, "Bugger

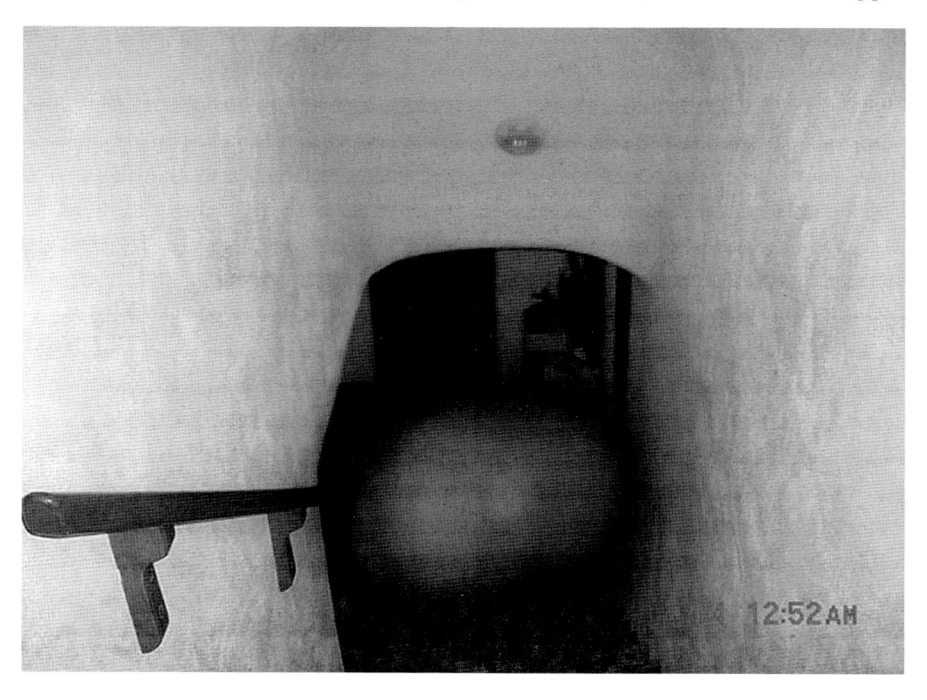

Unusual photo taken by the Ghost Patrol with Donovan in 2001. *Photo by the author.*

off, and put the lights back the way they were!" The bedside lamp turned off, and the light by the door turned back on. However, the ghost wasn't through with Bob. At six o'clock in the morning, the clock's alarm went off, despite the fact that Bob did not even bother to wind up the clock. It turns out that this was one of the phenomena many people have reported over the years.

The following morning, we were told the ghost story of George Daves and Cleopatra Edmunds. According to the story, Daves shot himself after Edmunds refused to marry him. His ghost supposedly haunts the property now. Our next investigation of the property occurred a year later, in October 2003. Again, we were with Donovan's Ghost Patrol. The strategy this time was to isolate female investigators to examine if anything unusual would happen to them if they were left alone in the rooms where previous female tenants had been harassed.

While this investigation was not very fruitful, there was one clear incident in which we recorded the sound of footsteps walking up the staircase. Cameras that were set up as controls clearly showed that no one was anywhere near the area when the steps were recorded.

A large number of unusual occurrences happen in the area around the stairs. *Photo by the author.*

Haunted Tombstone

Little did we know that another unusual experience occurred at the bed-and-breakfast a month after this visit. This one was reported to Josh Hawley at Tombstone Paranormal. I have chosen to include it here because of the multiple reports from visitors of similar experiences while staying at the Buford House:

> *In July 2002, Jolene and I traveled to Tombstone, Arizona, and stayed in the Buford House, a reportedly haunted bed-and-breakfast. Before this trip, I was extremely skeptical that ghosts really were anything other than the product of overactive imaginations. However, the events of that night changed my perspective completely.*
>
> *The Buford House is a plain, two-story adobe structure situated on a quiet street. The proprietors, Ruth and Richard Allen, are some of the nicest folks a person could ever meet. Our room was downstairs and had a private entrance with a little side porch where we could go to smoke. In their room were a double bed, a dresser, and a small sofa that converted into a bed. On the surface, nothing seemed unusual.*
>
> *We knew it was supposed to be haunted, having seen it featured on* Haunted History *on the History Channel. But, I really did not expect to experience anything.*
>
> *Richard took us on a tour of the home and gave us a brief history. He said he did not want to tell us too much about the ghosts and what they did because he did not want to influence us. (I thought, yeah, because there isn't anything to tell.)*
>
> *I don't remember exactly what time we went to bed, but it must have been about 11:00. I slept in the double bed, and she opened out the sofa and made her bed there.*
>
> *Later, I was awakened with a jolt. I mean an actual shock. I was lying on my stomach, sound asleep, when it felt like I was hit in the middle of my back with 220 volts of electricity. (Now this could not have been faked by the owners because my back was not on the mattress.) There was a tingling sensation running up my spine and down my legs, and I could not move. It was as if I was being held in place. Then the weirdest thing of all happened: I felt the covers being slid off my body—not to the floor, but toward the center of the bed. Someone (or something) was pushing the covers off me. Then I felt a hand stroking my backside. I still could not move.*
>
> *Jolene came to the bed and said someone had been calling her name so loudly, it woke her up. When she began talking to me, whatever it was that had me, let go. Both of us were scared witless. I got up, got fully dressed,*

and we spent the next two hours on the outside porch before we got enough courage to go back inside.

I did not tell Richard and Ruth about what happened to me because, at the time, I was embarrassed that the entity had touched my rear end. Now I can talk about it because I have had time to sort it out and realize, I have nothing to be embarrassed about.

Would I ever go back to the Buford House? In a heartbeat, only this time I would not be afraid. I think I would try to interact with who-or what-ever it was.

Paranormal incidents from other well-known people have been reported at the haunted bed-and-breakfast. Actor Bruce Boxleitner also had a rather strange experience while staying at the Buford house. The actor was in town to attend the first Tombstone Film Festival. The first night of his stay, he placed his wallet, watch and room key on the nightstand next to the bed. The following morning, he awoke to discover that his wallet was missing. Frantically, he began searching the room for his missing property. He looked in all of the drawers in the cabinets, around the bed and eventually started going through other pairs of pants that he had worn. Suddenly, he spotted the wallet sitting on a chair in plain sight. While he thought this was rather odd, he didn't think much about it afterward. Later that day, after returning from the film festival, he discovered his two boys arguing over some action figures that were missing. The trio began searching the room for the missing toys to no avail. Meanwhile, in his room, his wife discovered the missing action figures, which were tucked away in the top drawer where she was keeping her lingerie. Again, the experience seemed odd, but not much thought was put into it.

Later that evening, Bruce was up watching television while the rest of his family slept. He recalled that it was a rather hot night and that he simply was not sleepy. After watching TV for a while, he had started to drift off when the left side of his body suddenly became extremely cold. He also had the sensation that he was not alone in the room. Fully awake now, he looked up and noticed a shadow on the wall next to him. Before he could react, several loud noises, which sounded like someone stomping on the floor, came from the other side of the room. He bolted up out of the chair only to discover that he was alone in the room. No one was there.

Startled, he left the room and entered the hallway heading back toward the rear of the house. Surely there had to be a logical explanation, he thought, as he stood in the hallway. He looked up into a small mirror that hung on the wall just opposite the staircase. As he looked into the mirror, he suddenly became aware that someone was standing behind him. While the figure was dark, he could distinctly make out that this person was wearing attire very similar to what the reenactors wear in town. The most distinctive feature that he could make out was that the figure behind him was wearing a cowboy hat. He turned around to see who was behind him only to discover that no one was there.

The following morning, he went into the kitchen and talked with Richard. After Bruce told him about his encounter the night before, Richard related the story of George and Petra.

Ruth Allen, one of the owners of the house, actually saw the face of a man in December 1999. The apparition was in the front room of the house looking at the Christmas tree. When she saw the specter, it looked back at her and smiled. She wasn't frightened, she just accepted the ghost's presence. "We are open to it," she said. "We're optimistic skeptics."

In Search of the Truth

The tragic story of George Daves and Cleopatra Edmunds was sensational news in 1888. The *Tombstone Daily Prospector* published the story on April 14, 1888:

> He Blows His Brains Out and Dies at the Doorstep of Her House
>
> *At twenty minutes past two yesterday afternoon five pistol shots rang out clear and deadly, startling all who lived in the neighborhood of Second and Safford streets. Before the sound of the last shot had died away or the smoke from the pistol passed into the air, half a score of people had rushed to the scene of the shooting and there beheld a tragedy of unrequited love and death. The principals in this sad affair were George Daves and Miss Cleopatra Edmunds, a 17-year-old daughter of the well-known former citizen, Eugene ("Stockton") Edmunds, who died here several years ago. From all that could be learned it appears that Daves had for a long time been an ardent admirer of the young lady, and when he left here several months ago to better his position in life, it was, so he informed several of his intimate friends, with the understanding that upon his return they were*

to be married. He went to a mine about forty miles from Casa Grande and there worked steadily for some months until he believed he had accumulated sufficient wealth to begin married life with. With this intention, he returned to this city last Tuesday and immediately went to the residence of his intended, whose reception gave him no doubts of her continued affection.

Thursday evening they together visited a neighbor in company with several others had a pleasant time until the hour for departure, when to his surprise and mortification she rejected him and accepted the escort of another. After returning home, he told his father "It's all over. I want nothing more to do with that girl." What cruel doubts and maddening thoughts racked his brain during the vigils of the night no one will ever know, and when his father left him early in the morning, he yet tossed on his bed with sleepless eyes, saying he had not closed them all night. When his father returned at noon, he said his son acted as if he had the blues, and he concluded he would not go to work but would stay with him the remainder of the day. A few minutes before the shooting the boy walked to the front door, then immediately stepped back and saying, "Goodbye, father," picked up a revolver and quickly passed out into the street. Before his father could reach the door to halt or call him, he heard the shots and stepped into the street only in time to see his unfortunate son place the revolver to his head and send a bullet crashing through his brain.

The following account given by an eye witness a prominent and reputable citizen is not without interest. He said: "I was walking up Third street with a friend, and as we passed Edmunds' house I saw a young man standing on the outside of the fence talking with Cleopatra Edmunds; she being on the inside near the gate. We had not gone more than 100 yards when I heard a woman scream, followed by a pistol shot. Turning I saw the young woman running across the street from the direction of Daves' house, which is situated on the corner of Bruce and Third, about 80 or 90 feet diagonally across the street from Edmunds', followed by a young man who was firing at her as he ran. When she reached the front door of her house, she fell, and he raising the pistol to his head fired, and fell just outside and in front of the gate."

Another party who was also an eye witness, corroborates the above statement, adding, however, that the young woman walked across the street to the corner at Daves' house with the young man who was talking with her at the gate. That there she left him, and as she turned to return home, Davis came out of his house. Seeing him with a pistol in his hand she ran towards home, he following, firing four shots at her and taking his own life *with the fifth. Of the four shots fired at Miss Edmunds, one made a slight flesh wound on the top of the right shoulder, another entered the back just to the right of the lower point of the right shoulder blade, passing through the right lung and body and coming out at the left margin of the right armpit, making a dangerous and possibly fatal wound. Immediately after being shot she was attended by Dr. Goodfellow and at 12 o'clock last night was resting easy.*

George Daves placed the pistol to his right temple when he fired the suicidal shot, the bullet entering the head at that point and coming out at the crown, causing almost instant death.

Justice Shearer will hold an inquest on the body at 2 o'clock this afternoon, at Ritter's undertaking rooms. The funeral of the suicide will take place from the undertaker's rooms at 2 p.m., Sunday.

George Daves was 21 years old. He was born in Santa Clara Co., California and had lived here for the past five years. He has always been known as a quiet, peaceful and industrious boy. The deed he committed was the act of an irrational frenzied brain, his life and probably that of an innocent woman paying the penalty of his madness.

This article presents a problem with the ghost story. The Buford House is located on the south side of Safford Street, near the corner of Second Street. While the article starts out with the right location, by the third paragraph, it places the Daves house on Third and Bruce. This is a block north and another block east of the Buford House. The ghost story of the Buford House is dependent on the fact that George Daves and his father had lived in the Buford House on the south side of Safford between First and Second at the time of the tragedy. This is the reason that many people believe his spirit is still residing there. If this is not true, then the ghost haunting that property cannot be George Daves.

As I started to research this further, I discovered that research specialist Rita Ackerman had also found the discrepancy, and she took it several steps further. She looked at the court records for the inquest, Case No. 53, which was held on April 14, 1888. This document clearly defines the incident occurring on Third Street between Bruce and Safford. She then followed up this finding by analyzing the city plat map, deeds and tax records to determine that the Edmunds house was definitely located mid-block on the west side of Third between Bruce and Safford. She also was able to pinpoint the location of the Daves house on the northeast corner of Third and Safford Streets.

The area in the basement where human remains were found. *Photo by the author.*

So how did the Buford House become confused with the Daves house? Rita was also able to put the pieces together to show how the misconception started. Later in her life, Petra married Walter Lombardi. They lived in the house on the northwest corner of Safford and Second Streets, right across the street from the Buford House. The events in newspaper articles could be misinterpreted so that the location of the Daves house was the same as the Buford House but only if the actual locations are ignored, and the ghost story goes solely on the site of where Petra lived later.

While this may be quite disheartening to the psychics and mediums who have claimed to contact George Daves, it does not necessary debunk the reports of ghostly activity at the Buford House.

In October 2009, I visited the Buford House with Josh Hawley of Tombstone Paranormal. We were accompanied by 94 Rock, a radio station based out of Albuquerque, New Mexico. We were visiting the historical property to interview the residents and talk about the paranormal activity that has been occurring at the house over the past several decades.

While we were taking a tour of the house and listening to the various accounts attributed to the ghost, one of the owners mentioned that they

Haunted Tombstone

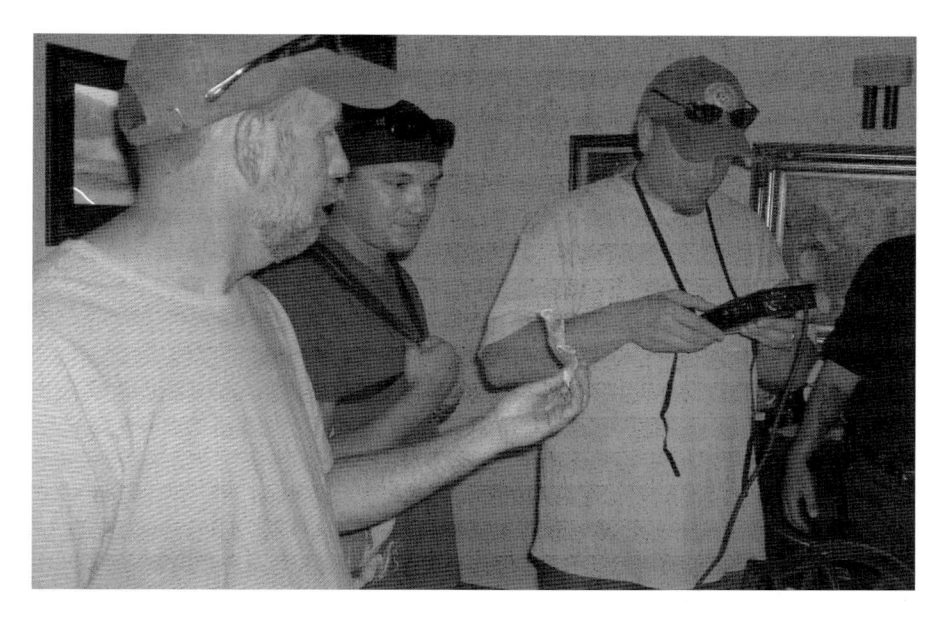

T.J. Trout examining the jawbone of a man found in the basement. *Photo by the author.*

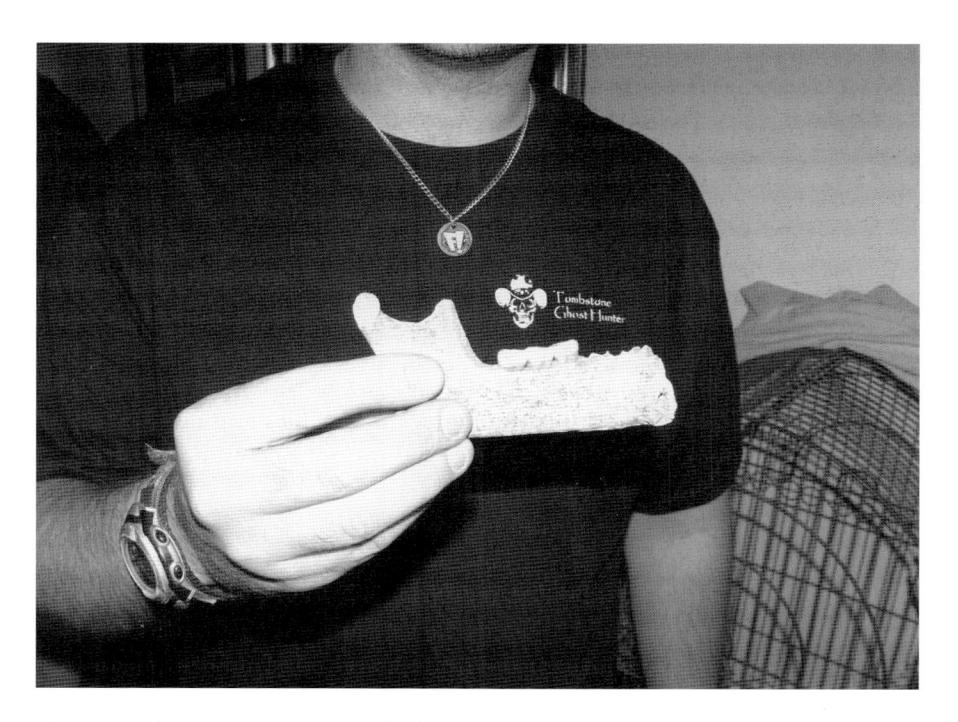

The human jawbone close up. *Photo by the author.*

The dug-out section in the basement where a human jawbone was found. *Photo by the author.*

had discovered human remains in the basement. We asked if the remains were still in the building, and to our amazement, we were informed that they still were. Within a few minutes, we were then led down the dark stairs and to the basement of the Buford House. Back in the corner of this small room, behind a partial wall that was mostly filled in with dirt, the owner pulled out a human jawbone. He had no idea how long this bone had been in the basement or if there were any more concealed somewhere in the basement's dark depths.

So now the Buford House has a mystery as well. How and when did the human bones end up in its basement? There is definitely something unusual going on in the house, as there are far too many reports from multiple witnesses. So perhaps the house is haunted; however, the spirit that haunts it is now unidentified, which in many ways is actually creepier than knowing who it is.

5
THE CRYSTAL PALACE SALOON

In 1879, Tombstone was nothing more than a few tents, rude huts and the rugged home of more than ten thousand citizens crammed together in the sprawling mining camp. The Crystal Palace Saloon was first called the Golden Eagle Brewery and featured excellent bock beer, a free lunch and a display of wild animals. The Golden Eagle Brewery was in business until a fire on June 22, 1881. A local saloon owner was pouring out a batch of bad whiskey when his cigar started the fire. On May 26, 1882, Tombstone again suffered another fire. It erupted in a water closet located in the rear of the Tivoli Saloon, destroying the original Golden Eagle Brewery building. Frederick Wehrfritz then built an imposing two-story building on the original site of the Golden Eagle Brewery, at the corner of the newly named streets of Fifth and Allen.

On July 23, 1882, the Crystal Palace Saloon opened its doors. The shining crystal ware and the friendly management soon had a monopoly on the prominent citizens of Tombstone who wanted the best drink. The Crystal Palace became the place most frequented by those individuals prominent in the business and social registers of Tombstone. To have an office on the second floor of this building was tantamount to having the best address in town. The rooms upstairs were crowded with those names now familiar to millions. The front office facing Allen Street was occupied by Virgil W. Earp. Virgil Earp was serving in the dual capacity as marshal of Tombstone and deputy U.S. marshal. The records reveal that his address in Tombstone was listed as the office building above the Crystal Palace, Fifth and Allen, Tombstone, Arizona Territory.

The Crystal Palace Saloon. *Author's collection.*

The adjacent office on the Allen Street side was occupied by the famed retired army surgeon Dr. George Goodfellow, a firm friend of the Earp brothers, destined to be remembered as Tombstone's greatest doctor. Dr. H.M. Matthews retained his office on the Fifth Street side with side entrance on that street. Dr. Matthews will be remembered for his part as coroner in the decision for the cause of death of Frank and Tom McLaury and William Clanton on the afternoon of October 26, 1881. Since business depended largely, if not entirely on the mines, it was possible at any hour to find the owners and managers in the Crystal Palace indulging themselves with the finest spirits obtainable. Mine officials, gunmen, prospectors, rustlers, lawyers, stagecoach bandits, cowboys, lawmen, gamblers, homesteaders and outlaws rubbed elbows day and night as they crowded along its long bar. Big Nose Kate, the girlfriend of Doc Holliday, was rumored to spend lots of time at the saloon as well.

The proximity of the Crystal Palace to Tombstone's leading commercial houses, coupled with its excellent décor and service along with gambling rooms created its success as Tombstone's finest, the best-appointed bar in a town of nearly a hundred saloons. The management in those early years wisely chose the course of action that kept the gambling games honest and the ruffians from making a slaughterhouse of the Crystal Palace.

A view into what the Crystal Palace was like in the 1890s can be gleaned from this *Tombstone Epitaph* article:

> *On Wednesday evening a most disgraceful scene was enacted in the Crystal Palace Saloon. A Mexican street walker was given enough whiskey to make her drunk, whereupon, urged on by the crowd of drunken men, she danced the "can-can," making disgustingly indecent exposures of her person. Notwithstanding the fact that two officers were present, one a city official and the other a precinct officer, and were "admiring" spectators of the unseemly exhibition, no arrests were made. These two officers disgraced themselves and their positions by being present at such an affair and making no effort to stop it. Among the crowd were also a lot of boys. If there is no ordinance on the subject, one should be passed by the City Council prohibiting the presence of women in saloons.*

From the 1920s to the 1940s, the constant, uncontrollable underground water forced the closing of the mines. It also destroyed Tombstone's boomtown prosperity, and its population dwindled to a fraction of its heyday. Through the years the Crystal Palace Saloon, which had bloomed in the town's prosperity, reluctantly shared its despair. The Prohibition Amendment finally closed the Crystal Palace. With gambling and drinking outlawed, the gaming tables, bar and back bar were removed. According to local legend, the famous mahogany Crystal Palace bar found its way to a Mexican Cantina which was consumed by fire two years later. Much of the glory was gone. The second floor had been removed, and the interior of the saloon, which had been known from Chicago to San Francisco for its elegance, had been altered and filled with twentieth-century trappings.

The Crystal Palace has served as a Greyhound bus station, warehouse, and as a movie theater. With the repeal of prohibition and the subsequent prosperity of the war and postwar years, the Crystal Palace was again doing business at the same location. In 1963, the Crystal Palace still was in business when Historic Tombstone Adventures, an organization formed to preserve and restore many of the town's legendary landmarks, purchased the world-famous bar. After accumulating all the old photographs and records that were available, the organization commissioned craftsmen to restore the Crystal Palace exactly as it had been in the turbulent days. The large, nearly room-length mahogany front and back bars were replicated to inch-by-inch specifications, using the old photographs. This was the only way it could be done, as the original blueprints had been destroyed years ago. The eagle-

Haunted Tombstone

Crystal Palace Saloon, Allen and Fifth Streets, 1940. *Library of Congress.*

bedecked wallpaper was custom made as symbolic of the historic building's original Golden Eagle Brewery name.

On the outside, the wooden sidewalks and overhang were restored around the building, and a false-front second story, authentic in measured detail, was built. The original Crystal Palace was a two-story building when it was constructed in 1879. It burned to the ground in the fire of 1882. It was rebuilt with only one story. Even the names of some of the more famous tenants were painted, in period style, on windows of the offices they occupied. The Crystal Palace today remains a symbol of the real Old West.

The paranormal activity here varies, depending on who you talk to. Many of the employees have seen ghostly cowboys waiting to be served at the bar. When the bartenders turn to take an order, they note that the phantom patron has mysteriously vanished. Guests have witnessed the ghosts sitting alone at the tables or on stage or moving in different locations near the bar. Other reported phenomena include unexplainable movement of objects to various places, lights that turn on and off by themselves and a gambling wheel that appears to spin of its own accord. Several photographs have supposedly captured the wispy likenesses of Tombstone's former residents.

When Donovan's Ghost Patrol visited the saloon, we talked with a bartender named Ron. He told us that the strangest thing that he had ever witnessed while working at the saloon occurred one afternoon when one of his friends came out of the restroom and told him that there was an old

The Crystal Palace façade, 1937. *Courtesy of the Library of Congress.*

man in there and he didn't look very good. He suggested that Ron should check up on him. The older gentleman would be easy to identify because he was wearing 1880s-style clothing. Ron thought that the man might be one of the local reenactors and proceeded back to the restroom to see what the issue was. However, when he reached the toilet, he discovered that it was completely empty. He investigated the other restroom, only to find out that it was empty as well. Confused, the bartender thought that the old man might have somehow made his way back by the cooler. A search of that area also revealed nothing. So Ron returned to the bar. He was busy cleaning up when he looked up and saw the old man standing in the hallway that led back to the restrooms. As he stared at him in astonishment, the man simply faded away. Other encounters with this particular apparition claim that the elderly man rises from a table and slowly walks to the restroom, or they say that they have seen him standing in the rear hallway. Other unusual phenomena that have been reported in the restrooms are that faucets turn themselves on and off and the toilets appear to flush on their own.

We were told by a psychic who had been inside the saloon that the building was haunted by three spirits that had chosen to remain earthbound because they were protecting a secret stash of money that was hidden in the basement. While this may seem entirely fanciful, it is worth noting that there could be some shred of truth to this. The *Arizona Daily Star* reported on a robbery at the Crystal Palace on February 1, 1938:

Robbers entered the historic Crystal Palace saloon here last night, blew the safe and emptied it of its contents, approximately $485 in cash, according to the estimate of Walter Lombardi, proprietor. The burglary occurred between 1 and 6 a.m. when no watchman was on duty.

Officers were summoned at 6 a.m. when the bartender discovered the robbery. Sheriff I.V. Pruit was on the job from Bisbee at once and assisted by Marshal Hal Smith and Deputy W.A. Tyler, made a thorough investigation.

Lombardi pointed out that two men were seen here yesterday answering the description of professional, safe crackers seen in Tucson last week, headed in this direction. A description of the men and their car was broadcast throughout the southwest.

The robbery was done neatly, the safe being covered with tablecloths from the Crystal Palace dining room to muffle the noise of the explosion. This is the second appearance of robbers here this month, the first attempt to rob the Southern Pacific safe proving unsuccessful.

The three safecrackers were captured in New Mexico a month later. However, the stolen money was never located. Later, one of the convicts mentioned that some of the money was hidden in a basement in Tombstone, although the exact location is still a mystery.

The basement itself seems to be quite a rather interesting part of the building. In 2010, the Tombstone Ghost Hunters captured a bottle flying across the basement on video. Local rumors claim that the mine shafts under Tombstone may be accessed through crawl spaces in the cellar. If that is true, perhaps the money is hidden there. However, I have saved the best story for last.

In 2005, I was involved in a video production about ghost hunting in Tombstone. We were visiting all of the famous haunts and a few of the lesser known ones as well. The last stop of the evening was the Crystal Palace Saloon, which the producer had arranged access to after it had closed for the night. The cast and crew were walking together down Allen Street from the O.K. Corral. The sight of seven ghost hunters—all wearing shirts that had our logo on them—being followed by a TV crew really made us stand out. As we approached the saloon, we caught the eye of a gentleman who was walking in the opposite direction on the boardwalk. He approached me and asked if we really were ghost hunters. I told him that we were. He then proceeded to tell me about a paranormal encounter that he had at the Crystal Palace. Unfortunately, we were short on time, as the production crew was rushing us to get on the site. I apologized and gave him my e-mail address, adding that I was interested in hearing about what he had encountered. Since he briefly mentioned something about seeing an apparition, I asked him to include as many details as he could remember and make a sketch if possible. The gentleman, whose name was Jeff, was very understanding. He promised to write and wished us luck with the video production. About a week later, I received an e-mail from Jeff. He described what had happened to him and included a beautiful sketch of the apparition he claimed to have seen. I contacted him later to get a more complete picture of what happened. Here is his story:

> *Me and six of my biker buddies came to Tombstone during Helldorado days in 2004. The first night we went to the Crystal Palace Saloon to have a few beers. We found a table in the middle of the floor near the wall and ordered our drinks. That was when I noticed this attractive woman on the other side of the room standing near the door. She was dressed in an old fashioned dress which was red with what looked like black lace accents. Around her chest, she wore something that resembled a red corset. She wore long fingerless gloves that came up to her elbows, and her dirty blonde hair was pulled up into a bun with a red feather stuck in it. On her right side, the dress was pulled up all the way to her hip and was fastened there by a piece of black lace or ribbon. She wore black stockings that came up to her midthigh. Showing that much leg, it definitely got my attention. My buddies soon noticed her as well, and she quickly became quite the distraction.*
>
> *About 20 minutes later we had finished our beers and had ordered another round. By this time it had become apparent that this woman was alone. No one, other than us, seemed to be taking any notice of her. She was just standing there, looking blankly around the room as if she was looking for someone. This was when one of my buddies, Ted, suggested that I should go over and invite her to come have a drink with us. This quickly became the topic of conversation as the suggestion turned into a bet. If I could get the lady to come over to our table, my friends would buy my beers for the rest of the evening. If I failed, then I had to buy everyone else a round. It sounded like a good deal to me.*
>
> *I got up and started walking in her direction, trying to think of the best strategy to convince her to come over. I decided on the "honest" approach.*
>
> *I walked up to her and introduced myself, immediately following that up with a brief description of the bet. I told her that there was a free drink in it for her, regardless if she stayed at the table or not. She just stood there. She*

didn't say anything or make eye contact. She seemed to be just staring off into space. Right when it started to get awkward, I heard someone nearby laugh and say something like "look at that ole boy talking to himself." A burst of laughter followed. I had an odd feeling that I was the source of the amusement. I turned to see a table with several locals, all dressed in Old western garb. Indeed, I was the one they were looking at. One of them yelled over at me, "You oughta lay off the hard stuff or pack it for the night." The rest of the cowboys laughed. I shrugged and laughed it off. I then turned back around only to discover that the lady had vanished. I quickly looked around the room, but she was nowhere to be found. My heart dropped. I had lost the bet, and now I was going to have to pay up. She must have ducked out the door somehow while I was distracted.

I started back to the table, expecting to be on the end of more laughs and taunting from my friends. However, the looks on their faces suggested something different. They looked astonished, almost as if they were in shock or something. Surely it couldn't be my picking up skills, as they have seen me turned down before.

When I reached the table, I was greeted by a barrage of questions and comments. "Did you see that?" "That was so freaky!" "That was crazy!" "I can't believe it!" "That was a real ghost, man!" I admit that I was quite puzzled. What were they talking about?

"That girl," they explained, "When you turned around she just vanished. Boom, gone!"

"No," I argued. "She wasn't a ghost, she was real. I was only about three feet away from her. She must have ducked out of the door."

I thought that they were messing with me, adding insult to injury. However, they were quite adamant that they all watched her "fade away" while I was distracted by the cowboys. Their reactions seemed genuine, but these guys were good at the game. No one at the table was scared, in fact, it was quite the opposite. My friends were acting like they were freaked out, but they were discussing what had happened with excitement. Then they remembered the bet.

I tried to utilize their belief that the woman was a ghost to my advantage. A ghost wouldn't count, would it? If so, how could they know that she was not actually sitting at the table, right now, and simply couldn't be seen by anyone? I was determined to try to squeeze my way out of the bet, and I still thought that they were pulling my leg. Then something dawned on me. Other people in the saloon could have seen her. What about the locals who were poking fun at me when I was over at the door trying to talk to that girl?

I brought the subject up hoping that perhaps this would resolve this ghost nonsense. Ted suggested, "Well let's go ask them," as he got up out of his chair. I stood and followed a few feet behind him as he approached their table.

"Hey, did you guys see my buddy trying to hit on that woman in the saloon girl outfit?" He pointed towards the area where the woman had been standing. The same guy that taunted me earlier let out a chuckle. "There wasn't anyone over there! He was talking to the wall. I definitely wouldn't let him drive tonight." A couple of the others at the table smiled and nodded in agreement. Ted thanked them and turned to walk by to our table. "Well isn't that something," he jeered. "They said they saw no one over there but you. They thought you were talking to yourself."

Well, that would explain why they were laughing at me. Suddenly, I was unsure of my own skepticism. This happened just over a year ago. My friends have never changed their story and state that what they saw was legit. Have you ever heard anything like this that has happened to other people?

Jeff's drawing of the woman that mysteriously disappeared. Did his group see one of the saloon's ghosts? *Author's collection.*

I replied to Jeff's e-mail. I told him that the early psychical researchers thought that apparitions were actually something they called veridical hallucinations. The term *veridical hallucination* expresses the recognition that the hallucination in question is genuine and not a dream or a product of fantasy. Second, veridical hallucination is used in parapsychology to denote a class of telepathic hallucinations. The German hallucinations researcher Edmund Parish divided the class of telepathic hallucinations into veridical and coincidental. If it were a veridical hallucination, it would explain why some people could see the woman while others could not. Regardless of what it was, it is definitely a fun ghost story.

6
Boot Hill Graveyard

Boot Hill was not the first cemetery in Tombstone. In fact, two others preceded it. The first was located about a mile south of town near the Grand Central mine. However, it was only in use for a short period, as mine tailings encroached on it and started covering some of the graves.

In 1879, the second cemetery was established just north of town on Fremont Street. This graveyard was about the size of a city block. Although this was empty space back then, today, the boundaries of this graveyard run north to south between Bruce and Safford Streets. Its east–west boundary was from Sumner to First Street. Today, this is the block where the local Circle K convenience store stands. A resident in Tombstone described this cemetery in 1891, recalling that several graves were enclosed by fencing and that there was a Masonic section.

Within a year, a new extension of this cemetery began toward the north on top of the hill. This left a vacant area without graves sitting between the two. After this expansion, the older area began to fall into disrepair and was ultimately abandoned in preference to the newer northern section.

Much later, Tombstone was reminded of the area's history as a cemetery when houses were being built on top of it. The excavations for new housing dug up several grave residuals and a few skeletons.

The cemetery on top of the hill is now all that remains. It was in use from about 1880, and within a few months, it had a multitude of grave sites. The McLaury brothers and Billy Clanton were buried here after being shot dead at the O.K. Corral gunfight. It is also quite organized with specific

The gift shop at Boot Hill. Originally, this was the entrance to the graveyard. *Wikimedia Commons.*

sections. It has a Jewish area on the northeast side of the hill and a Chinese space designated at the very north end, just beyond the boundary fence of today's Boot Hill. The Catholic section kept growing larger and eventually expanded toward the west.

However, Tombstone was growing, and new homes were being built closer and closer to the cemetery. The town government soon erected a new cemetery on the end of Allen Street and closed the graveyard on the hill on May 31, 1884. After that, the cemetery on the hill was merely referred to as the old cemetery.

This old cemetery became neglected as the years passed. The townsfolk eventually forgot about the graves and began using it as a dumping ground for debris. A few people knew of its existence but had forgotten its name. They simply referred to it as the little cemetery on the road to St. David.

The eventual restoration of Boot Hill began in 1923 with a man named Frederick Bechdolt. He was an author who had written several books on the Old West. While researching some of the local history and lore in Tombstone, he visited the old cemetery on the hill. He was appalled at the condition of the graveyard. Covered in the discarded trash, it was almost impossible to discern where any specific graves were. The only one that was still obvious was a gravestone with the name "Martin Peel." It was disconcerting to him that this part of history had not been preserved and was practically forgotten.

He reacted by writing to the editor of the *Tombstone Epitaph*, expressing his shock and disgust that the cemetery was desecrated and in such a state of disarray. He wrote to the local paper, emphasizing how "the historical and practically only remaining Boot Hill Cemetery in the West, was being neglected." This was the first time that the old cemetery was referred to as Boot Hill. The letter soon reached city hall, where it attracted a great deal of interest.

In 1925, the town acquired the assistance of the Boy Scouts to help clean up the graveyard. Another local man, Harry Macia, located several of the burial sites, including those of the McLaurys and Billy Clanton. There he erected a marker that read "Murdered on the Streets of Tombstone."

Bechdolt was still involved and returned in May 1925 to speak at the Tombstone Luncheon Club. His speech emphasized preserving the history of the cemetery, and soon afterward, more people came forward to volunteer their help. A local surveyor donated his time to locate the boundaries of

Boot Hill in 1940, before the construction of the gift shop. The crosses in the center of the photo were once streetlights that were donated during the early restoration efforts. *Library of Congress.*

the graveyard to be fenced in, and a fund was created to assist with the costs of clean-up and for a formal restoration plan. Although there was a lot of talk, the action was occurring at a much slower pace. Eventually, the interest in the old graveyard on the hill grew again, which can be seen in this short article published by *Tombstone Epitaph* on April 4, 1928:

> *It may be no more desirable than possible to whitewash the picturesque sins of some of the buried on Boot Hill. Halos and white robes would rest incongruously upon those wide hatted gentlemen of the flaring mustachios, the fierce eyes, and nervous trigger fingers. But at least the stones that cover them can be whitened. There they are, mound after mound row, the graves of old Tombstone's unknown. Roughly oblong heaps of earth and rocks, scores of them, 150, or 200, or even more of them. On a few, wild thorny shrubs have taken root. Stones litter all. Rocks are banked on the graves. Even the Earth is flinty, rough, barred, and grim. Forbidding is Boot Hill graveyard wherein lie the men who died with their boots on. Not a headboard, not a nameplate, nothing to identify any grave on all Boot Hill. Heavens above, could anything be more horribly symbolic? Here they lie, the bones of the gunman, the stage robbers, the cattle rustlers, the gamblers, painted Jezebels of the "cribs" and the dance halls. Yes, and among the lot may not lie a few others, people who died forlorn and friendless but were decent and self-respecting. The innocent suffer from the sinful with whom they are linked in life. And death also, at least on Boot Hill. Not a blade of grass in this Boot Hill graveyard. Not a flower nor a tree, nor anything soft, lovely and tender. Nothing but the barren ground rocks, thorny shrubs. Everything hard, flinty, drab, hard, ugly, sinister like the lives of most of those whose bones lie under the stony mounds that almost touch so close are they. There is a saddening appropriateness about it. All those lively, vigorous, brave, reckless, hard-hitting, hard-living, hard hating men and women who helped put color and life in the Tombstone of the early 80s have come to this. Nameless skeletons, side by side, row on row, on a stony, desolate hill.*
>
> *"Live hard and dangerously," said Nietzsche, the German philosopher. These people did, and see what came of it.*
>
> *Here are the "self-expressionists" of early Tombstone. Here is the "live your own life" crowd. Here is the jazz gang of the 80s who lived by their wits, or their six-shooters for their sex appeal. Here are the men of hot heads and soft hands, who would rather shoot it out than work it out or reason it out. Here are the boys who would rather take it from the other fellow*

Haunted Tombstone

An early photograph of the graveyard taken during the late 1930s. *Library of Congress.*

by force than earn it. Here is the saloon gang adhere and the dancehall habitués. Men and women who lived gaudy lives and were snuffed out.

In 1932, Highway 80, the "Broadway of America," was being constructed through Tombstone. In an odd twist of fate, the new highway actually cut through a part of the historic cemetery. Several graves were unearthed, and the occupants of the graves were quietly relocated to the new cemetery at the end of Allen Street.

Once the highway was completed, the town council knew that Boot Hill would be a great tourist stop. In 1933, the highway department gave permission to the town to construct a byway to the graveyard, which was identified by a six- by twelve-foot black-and-white sign that could be easily seen and photographed by passing tourists. It's new identity as a tourist attraction revived interest in the old graveyard. On April 6, 1933, the *Tombstone Epitaph* published this article.

Fifty years ago, Frank Vaughn, who has been a resident of Tombstone at intervals since that time and is again residing here, painted a wooden marker for the plot in Boot Hill cemetery where are buried McLowery [sic] and the Clanton brothers. The marker long since crumbled under the rays of the Arizona sun and a cross has been identifying the place during recent years.

> *Now, under the plans of the Chamber of Commerce for improvements at Boot Hill, Mr. Vaughn is to reproduce the marker in form and wording. Other changes are to include a marker of wood for the five Bisbee murderers hanged under the law by Sheriff ward and a clearing of a driveway around the outer edge of the plot outside of the Escapule fence.*

The restoration was still underway in 1933 and resulted in several exciting discoveries about the cemetery. As it turns out, the graveyard was much more massive than initially thought. An article in the *Tombstone Epitaph* on April 18, 1933, described what was discovered:

> *During the week, Dewey Chadwick, who has been in charge of a crew of workmen engaged in clearing and cleaning Boot Hill graveyard, counted the graves and found there are 259 outside of the drift fence, besides 17 excavations from which bodies have been removed. There may be seen here a small grave marked by a tumbledown stone bearing the name "Sam Harris." This is the only remaining grave in what was once the Jewish section of the cemetery, originally surrounded by an adobe wall. The wall long since disappeared without right or authority and the bodies all have been removed to other resting places with this one exception. On Monday, Harry Hughes, at work here, dug up a monkey wrench of antique design. It gives every evidence of having been buried beside one of the graves for approximately 50 years. It has been added to the collection of curios and the Chamber of Commerce offices.*

However, the popularity of Boot Hill soon began to threaten it, as souvenir hunters secretly carried away headstones and funeral markers. The graveyard was in need of a caretaker and some kind of fencing to protect the site. The fencing was erected out of branches of the ocotillo plant, which created a natural barbed wire fence that would deter the would-be robbers. The position of caretaker would be paid by concessions to be made from those who visited the graveyard.

In the 1940s, Emmett Nunnelly, a resident of Tombstone, began a significant effort to restore the cemetery to its original state. Harry Fulton Ohm, the owner of the Bird Cage Theatre, donated new steel markers from his plant to replace the wooden ones, which were already showing signs of decay. These are the same markers that remain in the graveyard today.

It is important to know that all of the graves are not marked in their exact locations. In fact, some of the graves could be from a couple of feet, one way or the other, but most are quite close to their exact location. Over the years, Boot Hill has been extensively studied and the graves not already marked with a headstone have been remarked as close to their original places as possible by using city records and charts.

Boot Hill has also been suggested as a possible location of hidden treasure. The August 2009 issue of *Lost Treasure* told of a small fortune of stolen loot that many believe is buried in or near the grave of Dutch Annie. The story goes that the Can Can restaurant was famous in its day for its food. It sold lobster and imported fish from Mexico and had a hired hunter who kept the café supplied with fresh meat. It was this man who stole a significant sum of money from the Can Can and was later caught. He said he buried the score not far from Boot Hill, but it was never found. The bandit died in jail before he could reveal the location.

The marker for the victims of the O.K. Corral gunfight in 1933. *Library of Congress.*

Of course, there are also the mysteries of the paranormal type. Visitors often report seeing strange lights and hearing unidentifiable noises coming from the old graveyard. With many reports of human-like shadows lurking from behind the bushes and misty figures ascending up from the graves as well as photos of unexplainable figures of people, no one really knows who these ghosts are or why many of them are there. Billy Clanton, who was killed in the Gunfight at the O.K. Corral, is said to rise from his grave before walking along the road back to Tombstone.

The manager of the Boot Hill Graveyard, Teresa Benjamin, tells people of her accounts of poltergeists and apparitions in the cemetery. She said the sweatshirt rack in the gift shop rotates on its own, money has gone missing and she has seen apparitions in photos taken of the graveyard. Pictures of Billy Clanton's tombstone are frequently reported to have unexplainable apparitions. Clanton was killed in the gunfight in 1881.

During the decades that I have spent investigating the paranormal claims of the town too tough to die, I have heard my share of strange stories about the old cemetery. However, this is one that I have always found fascinating.

Haunted Tombstone

It was told to me by a woman named Linda during a ghost-hunting retreat being held in Tombstone. This is her story:

My paranormal experience at Boot Hill was the most intense encounter that I have ever had. I would consider myself a "sensitive" of sorts. This often manifests as sudden dizziness that is followed by seeing something or someone that is indistinguishable move across a room. Almost like a shadow, but there is more substance to it. Occasionally, there are also unexplainable smells, like cigarette smoke in a place where there was no smoking allowed. Nothing real intense or tangible but like a perception of that odor.

This was my first trip to Tombstone, and my husband joked on the drive that I would probably be having some sort of physic experience every ten minutes during our stay.

Surprisingly, it was not that bad at first. The ghost hunting conference probably distracted me to some degree, and I had very little noticeable disturbances. That evening, the conference took us on a ghost tour through the town. One stop on this tour was the Boot Hill cemetery. Again, I really didn't feel anything. I have to admit that I was a little disappointed but there was always the next day since we had decided on spending the entire weekend there.

The following morning, we got up early and drove back out to Boot Hill. During the tour, it was closed, and the group was not allowed to go inside. I was anxious to see the grounds and to take photos of some of the more famous gravesites. After all, how can you come to Tombstone and not see Boot Hill!

We arrived way too early. The Visitor Center was not even open, so we decided to get out of the car and walk around the graveyard fence for a while until it opened. We were about fifty feet or so away from the parking lot when I noticed an Asian woman in a red dress walking around inside the graveyard. She seemed to be moving from one grave to the next, stopping and bending down for a brief moment before moving on again. At first, I thought that she was pulling weeds, picking up trash or perhaps putting something on the graves. This was when my husband saw her and remarked that the staff was probably out this early because it was safer to work early due to the rattlesnakes. Assuming that someone had arrived to open the Visitor Center, we started back. Just as we approached the parking lot, another car arrived, and a woman stepped out. She locked her car and went to open the front door. Walking to the entrance of the visitor center I suddenly felt dizzy and had to stop for a moment to let it pass. At first, I thought nothing of

Haunted Tombstone

The marker for the victims of the O.K. Corral gunfight as it appears today. Photo by the author.

it, and we walked into the Visitor Center and looked around. My husband decided to talk to the lone employee there about the snakes. While she did acknowledge that there have been sightings of rattlesnakes in the graveyard, she seemed confused when he mentioned the Asian woman that we had seen just moments earlier. She told him outright that she was the only one here and that there should not be anyone walking around outside. Naturally, we were suddenly curious about the person we had just seen outside. We left the gift shop and went into the cemetery. In general, I like cemeteries. They're peaceful and beautiful, and I enjoy the history. My husband and I walked the rows of grave markers and read from the pamphlet that described how the residents of the cemetery met their demise.

The side that was closest to the parking lot contained many of the graveyard's famous residents, and it was quite enjoyable; however, as we walked around we looked for the Asian woman, who was nowhere to be found. Then as we started to move across, I suddenly felt dizzy and out of breath. Halfway across the graveyard, I had to give my husband the pamphlet to read from because I felt weak and disoriented. We turned and

Haunted Tombstone

headed towards the top of the cemetery. I looked over at the headstone that belonged to someone called China Mary. Just as I started to read what was written on the pamphlet, I suddenly felt a turbulent wave crashing over me. I felt out of breath and had to kneel down. My husband was concerned, but I kept telling him I was okay. I just needed a minute to catch my breath. He gently teased me about angering the spirits and suggested that we should go. I told him that I was fine, and we moved to take a closer look at China Mary's grave.

Suddenly the dizziness hit like a wave again, churning. I felt like I was body surfing without the rest of my body. With each step, breathing became painful and difficult. I felt like someone was standing on my chest as there was this strange pressure. I am confident that it was not a medical situation. I had drunk plenty of water. I had opened a bottle on the way to the cemetery and finished it while walking around waiting for the Visitor Center to open. However, I have had enough. This was completely overwhelming. We started walking back towards the exit. With each step in the opposite direction, the feelings decreased by half. I took a handful of pictures there but haven't found anything unusual in them.

This photo was taken from a similar viewpoint as the 1940 photograph. A comparison between the two is very interesting. *Wikimedia Commons*.

My gut feeling is that I was sensing China Mary's spirit. She was a significant figure in Tombstone's history and a compelling woman. I knew nothing about her until this happened and I had researched some more information about her on the internet. According to something I had found online, she died of heart failure. So I guess that would explain the heaviness in my chest. Part of me really wanted to keep walking and see how far the experience would go. Could I pick something else up? But under the circumstances I just couldn't. The bizarre thing was that we never found out who the Asian woman was that we saw in the graveyard earlier in the morning. Perhaps it was the apparition of China Mary herself.

While I will admit that I am not a massive advocate of psychics and mediums, this is the fourth instance where I had witnesses describing an Asian woman in a red dress. Three of the sightings were during the daylight hours; the other was just after sundown. All four also had some sort of element that involved dizziness or the feeling of some kind of pressure on their chests. Is this really the restless spirit of China Mary or perhaps something else?

7
RED BUFFALO TRADING COMPANY

Bob Hatch and John Campbell opened a billiards parlor in 1880. Hatch was a colorful character and an amateur actor. It was said he kept a jar of frogs on the counter, as their croaking helped him predict the weather. Bob also followed the Earps to the famous gunfight and assisted in removing the gun from dying Billy Clanton's hand. He also testified at the hearing.

At 10:50 p.m. on March 18, 1882, Morgan Earp was shot through the body by an unknown assassin while playing a game of billiards. At the time the shot was fired, he was playing with Bob Hatch and standing with his back to the glass door in the rear of the room. The door opened out on an alley that led straight through the block along the west side of A.D. Otis and Company's store to Fremont Street. This door was an ordinary glass door with four panes in the top in place of panels. The two lower panes were painted, while the upper ones were clear. Anyone standing outside could look over the painted glass and see anything going on in the room. At the time the shot was fired, Morgan must have been standing within ten feet of the door, and the assassin, standing near enough to see his position, aimed for about the middle of his body, shooting through the upper portion of the unpainted glass.

The bullet entered the right side of the abdomen, passing through the spinal column, completely shattering it. It then exited his body on the left side, crossed the length of the room and lodged in the thigh of George Berry, who was standing by the stove, inflicting a painful flesh wound.

After the first shot, a second was fired almost immediately through the top of the upper glass. The bullet passed across the room and lodged in the wall near the ceiling over the head of Wyatt Earp, who was sitting watching the game. Morgan fell after the first shot and lived for only about an hour. His brother Wyatt rushed to his side and quickly moved him some ten feet away to get him out of the line of fire just in case another shot was fired.

Doctors Matthews, Goodfellow and Millar were called and examined him. After a brief consultation, they pronounced that the wound was mortal.

Morgan was then moved into the card room and placed on the lounge, where he breathed his last breath. He was surrounded by his brothers—Wyatt, Virgil, James and Warren—and the wives of Virgil and James and a few of his most intimate friends. Despite the intensity of the pain from the gunshot, he did not complain.

Morgan Earp. Does his ghost really haunt the location of his death? *Wikimedia Commons.*

The saloon and billiard parlor burned in the 1882 fire and was one of the first to be rebuilt. Prohibition closed all the saloons in 1914. This area deteriorated badly in the following years, but in 1945, this old building was remodeled for a new business.

Campbell and Hatch's is now a tourist shop called the Red Buffalo Trading Company. The shop primarily sells western antiques and attire to the tourists who want a souvenir from the town too tough to die. The significance of the building is announced by a window etching and a 2005 plaque outside the building, which reads:

> *Historic Location 19*
> *Morgan Earp was murdered while playing pool at Campbell and Hatch's Saloon on March 18th, 1882.*

Though the original building has been reduced to ashes in one of the many Tombstone fires, the location where Morgan Earp spent a lot of his waking hours in life is still frequented by him in death.

Haunted Tombstone

As with many of the haunted locations in Tombstone, the descriptions of paranormal activity here vary, depending on who is telling the stories.

Many people have sighted a female apparition they believe is the ghost of Morgan Earp's wife, who is searching for her deceased husband even in death. This explanation seems impossible, because she accompanied her husband's remains back to California, where he was buried. It is entirely possible that there is a female specter here that people are merely misidentifying. Other witnesses claim that the ghost haunting this building is Morgan Earp himself. He is commonly seen in the back corner of the building where he died.

Common phenomena, other than the occasional apparition, include the sound of footsteps walking around the rear of the Red Buffalo Trading Company and objects being moved or manipulated.

One story that is told to guests on the local ghost tour tells of the helpful ghost of Morgan Earp. Employees claim that Morgan watches over the store in their absence. At night, when everyone has gone home for the evening, Earp will face shelves, incorrectly, and tidy up the place. One employee is said to have been unable to finish stocking shelves before the store closed. Planning on completing the task in the morning, he left the box of wares still half-full. The last person there was the first at the shop in the morning, and when the employee went back to finish emptying the box, it was empty. The items that were in the box had been removed sometime during the night. However, the items were not shelved correctly, and the employee spent a lot of time trying to find where the cooperative spirit had set the box's contents.

Another suspect for this particular ghost could be George Berry. Berry eventually died after being shot that fateful night. However, Dr. Goodfellow said it wasn't the bullet that killed Berry. He said the man was scared to death.

Local photographer James Kidd claims to have unknowingly captured a somewhat unusual image on 35mm film while photographing an empty stage in the back for insurance purposes.

The distorted images of two women and one man are visible, both wearing clothing from Tombstone's heyday. One woman appears to be wearing a large hat. The man may have sideburns and wears a buttoned-up coat.

The blurring in the image was confined to this one frame. The frames occurring before and after have no unusual qualities in them. The area where this photograph was supposedly taken is close to the place where Morgan Earp died.

Haunted Tombstone

The location of the negative for this photo is not known, preventing a full analysis of the picture. However, the effects seen in the picture suggest issues with the aperture settings and possibly development or camera malfunction problems, so it is somewhat hard to say what is actually in the photograph. Regardless, many people claim to feel the presence of some supernatural force inside the building.

8
O.K. CORRAL

The O.K. Corral (Old Kindersley) was a livery and horse corral that was located in Tombstone from 1879 to about 1888. The purpose of a livery was to provide public transportation and care of livestock. The majority of the residents of Tombstone did not actually own a horse. So when they needed to go out of town, they rented a horse from one of the liveries or corrals. The corrals and liveries also provided carriages and wagons with teams of horses.

According to testimony given to the inquest after the gunfight, the Cowboys left their horses at Dexter's Livery Stable and went to Spangenberg's gun shop on Fourth Street. Wyatt Earp saw them inside and later said he believed that they were filling their cartridge belts with bullets. The Cowboys then walked over to the O.K. Corral, where witnesses overheard them threatening to kill the Earps. Citizens reported the threats and the armed Cowboys' movements to Tombstone city marshal Virgil Earp.

On April 19, 1881, the city had passed an ordinance that required anyone carrying a bowie knife, dirk, pistol or rifle to deposit their weapons at a livery or saloon soon after entering the town. Virgil Earp believed that the Cowboys had violated this ordinance, which led to his decision to confront them. The tense environment escalated the situation and resulted in the shootout.

The Earps and Doc Holliday walked west on Fremont Street to confront the Cowboys. After passing the rear entrance to the O.K. Corral, they found the Cowboys gathered in a narrow, twenty-foot-wide lot that was

Haunted Tombstone

The location where the apparition of Justice Jim has been reported. *Photo by the author.*

The display of the gunfight near Fremont Street. *Photo by the author.*

adjacent to C.S. Fly's boardinghouse and photography studio. The gunfight took place within the small lot and on Fremont Street and lasted about thirty seconds.

At the time of the famous gunfight on October 26, 1881, the O.K. Corral was one of seven liveries and corrals in the town and was owned by John Montgomery and Edward Monroe Benson. The corral and surrounding buildings were entirely destroyed by a fire on May 25, 1882. The corral was rebuilt when the site began to gain attention from the American public in 1931, the year author Stuart Lake published a biography of Wyatt Earp. Although it was highly fictionalized, the book quickly captured imaginations of the American people and soon became the basis for the 1946 film *My Darling Clementine*, which was directed by John Ford.

In 1957, the film *Gunfight at the O.K. Corral* was released, fixating the connection of the gunfight to the corral itself. The corral was bought by investors from Detroit, Michigan, led by attorney Harold O. Love. The Love family owns the O.K. Corral today.

However, there was another gunfight at the O.K. Corral. This one occurred on July 1, 1897. It involved a rather colorful character in Cochise County at that time, a man named "Justice" Jim Burnett. Burnett was a New Yorker who was born in 1832. He was associated with the Charleston and San Pedro River area for over twenty-five years. One of the earliest mentions of him was in the *Arizona Republican* newspaper in July 1879. He was holding a coroner's inquest over the body of Dennis Consadine, a local troublemaker whose body was riddled with knife wounds and bullet holes in the chest. Such scenes would appear throughout Burnett's career.

He also was a man who wore many hats. He was a rancher, farmer, justice of the peace, coroner, butcher and livery operator. However, he is mostly remembered for his association with the town of Charleston and with his role as justice of the peace.

The Burnett ranch was located on the San Pedro River near Hereford. His neighbor was a man named William Cornell Greene. The two men honestly hated each other, as they were regularly competing for the water of the San Pedro River.

In 1897, Greene placed a small dam on the San Pedro River just above his ranch. Burnett's ranch was downstream, but he had enough water for everyday pasture needs. However, Burnett decided to expand his operation and hired a Chinese crew to build a different dam. He also gave instructions that if his ranch needed more water, they were to blow up Greene's dam, and if he did anything about it, Burnett would merely kill him.

Sometime during the night of June 24, 1897, Greene's dam was blown up, and the water was released. Unfortunately, Greene's two daughters, Eva and Ella, and their friend Katie Corcoran received permission to go to their favorite swimming hole to cool off. Katie jumped into the supposedly shallow pool and went to the bottom. Ella jumped in, realized the sudden change in depth, and yelled to her sister to "Go back, go back!" Eva went for help, but it was too late. Ella Greene and Katie Corcoran drowned because the swimming hole had been enlarged from the destruction of the dam.

Overwhelmed with grief, Greene placed an ad in the *Tombstone Prospector* on June 28:

> *$1000 REWARD*
> *I WILL PAY $1000 REWARD FOR PROOFS*
> *OF THE PARTY OR PARTIES, WHO BLEW*
> *OUT MY DAM AT MY RANCH ON THE NIGHT*
> *OF JUNE 24, THEREBY CAUSING THE DEATHS*
> *OF MY LITTLE DAUGHTER AND KATIE CORCORAN*
> *W.C. GREEN* [sic]

Greene's ad soon had a reply, and he learned about Burnett's orders to destroy his dam from a Chinaman named Ah On. Confident that he knew who was responsible for the girls' deaths, he went looking for Burnett.

He finally found him on July 1. Burnett was on Allen Street, near the O.K. Corral. Green approached him and drilled Burnett with three revolver shots, killing him almost instantly.

The shooting was the talk of the town on July 2, 1897. The *Arizona Republican* ran the following short story:

> *Marshal Meade received a dispatch from Tombstone which said, "Bill Greene killed Jim Burnett here today." There were no further particulars, but it is believed at the Marshal's office that another death had led to the tragedy of today. About a week ago a dam on the San Pedro owned by Mr. Greene was blown out. It so happened that a little daughter of Mr. Greene's was playing in the river below with a companion from Bisbee, and in the rush of the water which followed the blowing up of the dam, both children were drowned. Greene offered a reward of $1000 for information that would lead to the discovery of the party who had blown up his dam and thus brought death in his family, and it is believed to be the sequel of today's killing.*

Greene surrendered to Chief of Police Charley Wiser, who then turned Greene over to Sheriff Scott White. The only statement Greene gave was, "I have no statement to make other than that man was the cause of my child being drowned." As the public interest in the case developed, the same paper released more information two days later.

> *Greene's statement taken from the Tombstone Prospector's report of the inquest:*
> *The most important witness sworn was John Montgomery who testified that when Mr. Greene came into town with Mr. Scott White, he came to his stable and asked that his team be put up and also left a pistol with him. I locked it up and later, just before the shooting, probably two hours later, he asked me if there was anyone working in Hart's old shop. He sat in a chair until I went and got the pistol. He apparently started, as I supposed to the shop, but he did not put the gun in his pocket as far as I saw. He turned around by the corner of the office and accused Jim Burnett of having his dam blown up. Burnett made a denial in words, and then there were three shots fired, and Burnett fell.*
> *Both men are well known throughout the county having been pioneers before the creation of Cochise County. Burnett at the time of his death was Justice of the Peace at Pearce and owned a ranch on the San Pedro near the ranch of W.C. Greene.*

Greene, Wiser and White actually were close friends, and they had a shared dislike of Burnett in many ways. On July 8, 1897, the *Arizona Republican* ran a somewhat unusual article. It read:

> *Last Thursday in Tombstone William C. Greene of the San Pedro, shot and killed James C. Burnett. Mr. Greene claims that he ascertained beyond the shadow of a doubt that Burnett had occasioned the blowing up of his [Greene's] dam on the San Pedro, thereby causing a rush of water which overwhelmed and drowned his little girl and her companion Edna Cochran [sic]. Mr. Green also claims that Burnett had at different times threatened his life. It is known that there had been ill feeling between the two men, who own neighboring ranches below Fairbank. The* Tucson Star *states that Burnett bore a bad reputation and is said to have killed several men.*
> *However that may be, Burnett was a man who was much given to threatening and whose name came before a good many grand juries. If Mr. Green is able to show good reason for believing that Burnett was responsible for the blowing out of his dam and the consequent death of his child and*

can also show as he claims that Burnett had threatened his life but a few minutes before the shooting there will be a strong tide of popular sentiment in favor of the defendant.

His preliminary trial was set for Saturday, but on account of the illness of District Attorney English was postponed till today.

In the subsequent circus-like trial in Tombstone, Greene was acquitted.

Another version of the Burnett killing comes from Joseph Axford's book *Around Western Campfires*. Axford claims that after Greene discovered the death of his daughter, he immediately rode out of Cananea, Mexico, for Tombstone. When he arrived in town at the O.K. stables, he found Burnett in the office, seated in a chair talking to John Montgomery. Greene got out of the coach, and as he approached Burnett, Burnett threw his hands back to get up from the chair and Greene shot him just as he stood up, killing him instantly. Greene, raising his hand over Burnett's body, said, "God's will be done," and turning, walked down to the courthouse and surrendered to Scott White, the sheriff. His bail of $500,000 was paid the next morning. He was tried and found not guilty. The jury believed that when Burnett threw his hands back, Green had thought that Burnett was going for his gun, making the killing a case of self-defense.

Today, the O.K. Corral is believed to be haunted by the ghosts of the Cowboys. Over the years, there have been a multitude of witnesses who have claimed to have felt numerous cold spots and various sightings of the apparitions of several men dressed in cowboy attire in multiple areas of the corral. These specters are often reported as appearing with their guns drawn, which has led to the speculation that the ghosts are those of the Cowboy faction, somehow locked into a perpetual battle with the Earps.

The manager of the corral, Douglas Clay, has said that he saw the ghost of a tall, thin man in a flat-brimmed hat enter the old office building, but when he went in, it was empty.

For many years, people have reported hearing the sounds of phantom horses coming from inside of the corral. However, Tombstone Paranormal discovered that the sounds were coming from a galloping horse ride that sits inside the corral.

It appears that most of the ghosts are around the O.K. Corral as opposed to inside of it. Several people have claimed to have seen a ghost standing on the corner of Third and Fremont Streets that they believe is Billy Clanton. Again, this may be because this area is close to where Billy died after he was shot during the infamous gunfight.

Inside the O.K. Corral. Photo taken during a ghost hunt in 2009. *Photo by the author.*

One of the most commonly reported apparitions is that of a balding old man with a peppered beard. Also seen mostly outside of the corral on Allen Street, he is believed to be the restless spirit of Justice Jim Burnett. He usually appears only momentarily and vanishes when people try to approach him.

My encounter also took place just outside of the corral. One evening, I was with several other ghost hunters, including Polo Cisernos, who at that time was the producer for Donovan's radio show at 93.7 KRQ and a member of the Ghost Patrol. We were in Tombstone to record several segments for Ghost Patrol later that evening. While we were waiting for Donovan to arrive, we were walking up and down Allen Street, investigating the claims of a woman in white who is said to be the ghost of a brothel madam who was unjustly hanged. As we were walking by Big Nose Kate's Saloon, a police vehicle drove past us on Fourth Street. The officer would pause momentarily and shine his spotlight in windows and darkened doorways, ensuring that the neighborhood was safe. We had been watching for a few moments when my fellow investigator Bob Carter had a brilliant idea. Why don't we ask the police officer about these claims? If anyone knew what was happening on the streets of Tombstone in the middle of the night, the police would.

So we approached the police car and struck up a conversation with the officer. It turns out that the officer was actually a deputy from the Tombstone Marshal's Office. Deputy Nash was very professional and polite as he addressed our questions about the woman in white and the common occurrences that happen in the evening after Allen Street shuts down. Not only did he tell us that neither he nor anyone else that he had talked to had not seen this ghostly woman, but he also thought that the story was made up. We thanked him for the information and were about to leave when he stopped us.

"Would you guys be interested in taking a look at the jail? There is something strange about it. A lot of us got an uneasy feeling in there at night. Sometimes we hear footsteps coming from the jail cells when we know nobody is in them. The basement is kinda freaky too."

Bob was excited—Polo not so much. Apparently, the idea of going to a jail cell was unappealing, regardless of the reason for it. However, he was outnumbered, and soon we were following Deputy Nash back to the marshal's office.

The office itself was located directly behind the old city hall building. The O.K. Corral was directly behind that. This is one of the reasons that Deputy Nash thought that the unexplainable footsteps and sensations were paranormal. Perhaps it had something to do with its proximity to the O.K. Corral?

We began by searching the office and jail cells for anything unusual that could be making the noises that the deputy described. We also looked for any significant electromagnetic fields, because at that time they were believed to create many of the symptoms the officers were describing. The only ones we located were A/C fields associated with electrical equipment. The one exception was a strong D/C field that measured eight milligauss that appeared to have a point source originating from the floor in the rear office. The old basement lies beneath this part of the building, so we moved the search downstairs. The section where we picked up the EM field in the room above was primarily used as an evidence locker. However, this area is flooded with other A/C fields coming from electrical wiring, making it more difficult to measure the D/C field with the equipment we had.

A couple of hours later, we were no closer to finding any rational explanations for the sounds that were being heard in the jail cells. Bob suggested that the noises could be originating from outside and were merely being heard in the area of the jail cells. So the group headed outside, where we split into two teams. Bob and Polo headed for the old city hall building

The public entrance to the O.K. Corral. *Photo by the author.*

to search for clues while I headed back around the block to the front of the O.K. Corral. We agreed on a rendezvous point, the old city park, which was located right next to the O.K. Corral.

I searched for awhile but didn't find anything that could be causing the sounds the deputy had described. So I walked over to the city park to wait for Bob and Polo and sat down at the picnic table closest to the corral. I had been waiting only a few minutes when suddenly I heard the sound of footsteps right behind me. I turned around expecting to see someone, and the noise stopped. Nobody was there.

I turned back around toward the table, and after a few seconds, the sound happened again. This time it was faster, like several quick footsteps. Again I turned around, and it stopped. Yet there was still no one there. Curious now, I started to look for an explanation for the noises I was hearing. Perhaps it was an echo of something off the O.K. Corral wall? The strangest thing is that it seemed to start when I was looking in a different direction and stopped when I turned around. I turned around again, but this time nothing happened. I stood up and walked over toward the wall. The noises seemed to be coming from nearby, very close to me, but I couldn't locate the origin of the sounds. So I decided to sit back down in the same place as before to see if it would happen again.

 I sat there for about ten minutes and was about to get back up when the footsteps materialized again. Instead of turning around, I focused on listening, trying to determine their exact location relative to my position. Indeed, they sounded like they were very close, and the steps were getting louder, as if they were approaching me. Suddenly, something grabbed my right hip, almost as if an unseen thing was trying to grasp the area where my gun would be if I were actually carrying one. I jumped up and spun around quickly. Of course, no one was there. Then I felt the same sensation on my hip. I reached down, only to discover that the recurring vibrations on my hip was my phone. I had muted it but left it on vibrate. So no ghostly grabbing. Honestly, this really startled me, and that does not happen very often. I was fortunate that my friends were not there to see it.

 I answered the phone. It was Bob informing me that Donovan had arrived and we needed to get to the Buford House as soon as possible. So in the end, I never figured out what was going on outside the wall of the O.K. Corral. So if you ever find yourself in the city park after dark, I would suggest looking by the wall of the corral, but you may want to turn off your phone.

9
THE STREETS OF TOMBSTONE

The streets of Tombstone are said to be haunted by several lingering ghosts from its violent past. However, lawlessness was not the only cause of untimely deaths in Tombstone's bloody history. Two terrible fires scorched the town, the first in June 1881 and a second in May 1882. During these two devastating fires, more than forty people lost their lives in the crowded saloons and brothels when they were suddenly caught in the inferno. Significant areas of the business district burned to the ground and were erased from history in a matter of minutes. The victims of these tragic events are rumored to make themselves known on occasion. Some people have reported seeing apparitions, complete with severe burns on their faces. Others have reported the smell of smoke and burning wood when there is no explainable reason.

The corner of Fifth Street and Allen is the haunt of one of the most often seen ghosts on the streets of Tombstone. Witnesses describe this specter as an older man dressed in a knee-length coat and wearing a black hat. The man limps awkwardly and crosses the street from the Oriental Saloon toward the Crystal Palace Saloon. In some accounts, the man falls to the ground in the middle of the intersection and then just vanishes. Because of the general description and the location, many believe that this is the ghost of Virgil Earp.

After the Gunfight at the O.K. Corral, the Earps relocated their families to the Cosmopolitan Hotel for protection. On December 28, 1881, around 11:30 p.m., three men who were hiding in an unfinished building across

The corner of Fifth Street and Allen, looking east. *Photo by the author.*

Allen Street ambushed Virgil as he walked from the Oriental Saloon to the hotel. Virgil was hit in the back and left arm by three loads of buckshot from about sixty feet. The Crystal Palace Saloon, which was behind Virgil, was struck by nineteen shots. Three passed through the window, and another passed a foot over the heads of several men who were standing by a faro table. Severely wounded, Virgil staggered into the hotel.

Dr. George E. Goodfellow removed four inches of shattered bone from Virgil's left arm, leaving his arm permanently crippled, and twenty buckshot from his side. Virgil was also shot through the back above the hip; the bullet penetrated his body and lodged near the hip bone above the groin.

The one problem with the rumored ghost being Virgil Earp is that Virgil died on October 19, 1905, in Goldfield, Nevada. However, there is no shortage of possible suspects, as the intersection of Fifth and Allen is known as the deadliest corner of the Wild West. Over thirty documented killings happened at this intersection. From that list, here are the two most probable suspects.

At this location, Luke Short shot Charlie Storms. Luke Short was a twenty-six-year-old faro dealer. Charlie Storms was a sixty-year-old professional gunfighter and gambler who had only been in town a few days. The cause of their dispute was simply the turn of a card.

Haunted Tombstone

The corner of Fifth Street and Allen, looking west. *Photo by the author.*

On Friday, February 25, 1881, Short was serving as the lookout, seated next to the dealer at a faro game in the Oriental, when he was involved in what became a well-known gunfight. His opponent was Charlie Storms. Bat Masterson, who was in Tombstone at the time, described what happened in a magazine article he wrote in 1907:

> *Charlie Storms and I were very close friends, as much as Short and I were, and for that reason, I did not care to see him get into what I knew would be a very serious difficulty. Storms did not know Short and, like the bad man in Leadville, had sized him up as an insignificant-looking fellow, whom he could slap in the face without expecting a return. Both were about to pull their pistols when I jumped between them and grabbed Storms, at the same time requesting Luke not to shoot, a request I knew he would respect if it was possible without endangering his own life too much. I had no trouble in getting Storms out of the house, as he knew me to be his friend. When Storms and I reached the street, I advised him to go to his room and take a sleep, for I then learned for the first time that he had been up all night, and had been quarreling with other persons. I was just explaining to Luke*

> *that Storms was a very decent sort of man when, lo and behold! There he stood before us, without saying a word, he took hold of Luke's arm and pulled him off the sidewalk, where he had been standing, at the same time pulling his pistol, a Colt's cut-off, 45 calibre [sic], single action; but like the Leadvillian, he was too slow, although he succeeded in getting his pistol out. Luke stuck the muzzle of his pistol against Storm's heart and pulled the trigger. The bullet tore the heart asunder and, as he was falling, Luke shot him again. Storms was dead when he hit the ground.*

The shot fired by Short at point-blank range set Charlie's shirt on fire. Tombstone physician George E. Goodfellow was only a few feet from Storms when he was killed:

> *In the spring of 1881, I was a few feet distant from a couple of individuals, (Luke Short and Charlie Storms) who were quarreling. They began shooting. The first shot took effect, as was afterward ascertained, in the left breast of one of them, who, after being shot, and while staggering back some 12 feet, cocked and fired his pistol twice, his second shot going into the air, for by that time he was on his back.*

Short was arrested by Tombstone city marshal Ben Sippy for the murder of Storms. During the preliminary hearing, Masterson testified that Short acted in self-defense and Short was released.

The second most probable suspect is "Billy the Kid" Claiborne. After the real Billy the Kid was killed, Billy Claiborne insisted everyone call him "Billy the Kid."

"Buckskin" Frank Leslie was tending bar at the Oriental Saloon on November 14, 1882, when Claiborne, who was very drunk, began using insulting and abusive language. Leslie asked Claiborne to leave, but Claiborne continued his foul and abusive speech. Leslie later told his side of the story to the *Tombstone Epitaph*:

> *I was talking with some friends in the Oriental Saloon when Claiborne pushed his way in among us and began using very insulting language. I took him to one side and said, "Billy, don't interfere, those people are friends among themselves and are not talking about politics at all, and don't want you about." He appeared quite put out and used rather bad and certainly very nasty language towards me. I told him there was no use of his fighting with me, that there was no occasion for it, and leaving him I joined my*

friends. He came back again and began using exceedingly abusive language, when I took him by the collar of his coat and led him away, telling him not to get mad, that it was for his own good, that if he acted in that manner he was liable to get in trouble. He pushed away from me, using very hard language, and as he started away from me, shook a finger at me and said, "That's all right Leslie, I'll get even on you," and went out of the saloon.

Within several minutes, two men told Leslie that there was a man waiting outside to shoot him. When Leslie stepped outside, he saw "a foot of rifle barrel protruding from the end of the fruit stand." He told Claiborne, "Don't shoot, I don't want you to kill me, nor do I want to have to shoot you." But Claiborne, who was still drunk, raised his rifle and fired, missing Leslie. Leslie immediately returned fire and hit Claiborne in the center of his chest. "I saw him double up and had my pistol cocked and aimed at him again....I advanced upon him, but did not shoot, when he said, 'Don't shoot again, I am killed.'" Claiborne was taken to a doctor by friends, where he died six hours after being shot. His last words were reportedly, "Frank Leslie killed Johnny Ringo, I saw him do it." He was buried in Tombstone's Boot Hill Cemetery. Leslie was found to have acted in self-defense and not charged with the death.

The ghosts of Tombstone are not confined to Allen Street either. In 2007, I was doing a paranormal convention in Tombstone at Schieffelin Hall. Later that day, after the presentations were done, one of the attendees, a woman from Phoenix named Carol, told me about an experience she and her friend had several years ago when they first visited Tombstone:

I first came to Tombstone with my friend Janice. After spending the day doing the typical tourist stuff, we went out to go bar hopping. After a few hours it was starting to get late, and the bars in town started closing. We had been at the Crystal Palace having drinks when we decided to walk back to our RV to turn in for the night. As we were walking, we became fascinated by how different the town "feels" at night time. So we decided to wander around and look at several of the places that we had visited during the day. We were walking down Toughnut Street when Janice grabbed my arm. "Somebody is following us," she whispered. I told her not to worry about it. After all the bars were closing, and it was probably someone else on their way back home. I turned and saw what looked like a man, but it really wasn't. It was more of a dark shadow that had a human shape. I could see lights through it, yet it appeared to be walking. What the hell was it? I'll admit that I was startled a little so we turned north onto First Street to see if it would follow us. The "shadow" walked out into the middle of the street, stopped and then just vanished.

When Carol got back home, she did a little research and discovered that the intersection of First and Toughnut was where John Wesley Heath was lynched. She is convinced that what she saw was his apparition.

In the early 1880s, John Wesley Heath was living in Arizona. For a short time, he served as a deputy sheriff in Cochise County, but he soon discovered that the pay was not to his liking. In November 1883, Heath moved to Bisbee with James "Tex" Howard. Along the way, Heath met several of Howard's friends: Dan "Big Dan" Dowd, Omer W. "Red" Sample and Daniel "York" Kelly. Together, the five men plotted a crime that would eventually become known as the Bisbee Massacre.

In its early years, Bisbee did not have a bank, and it was common knowledge that the $7,000 cash payroll for the Copper Queen Mine was delivered to the Goldwater and Castaneda Mercantile store one or two days in advance of the company's payday on the tenth of each month. Heath and his four companions planned to rob the payroll after it had arrived at the store.

The group rode to Frank Buckles's ranch, about ten miles outside Bisbee, where Heath immediately partnered with a local man named Nathan Waite and prepared to open a new dance hall. Heath and Waite opened their dance hall behind the Goldwater and Castaneda Mercantile general store on December 8, 1883. Later that evening, the outlaws rode into Bisbee. Waite would join the other four men while Heath remained at his saloon. The group tied their horses at the end of Main Street near the Copper Queen Mine smelter and calmly sauntered to the Goldwater and Castaneda store. Three of the bandits entered the store while the other two remained outside as lookouts. All of the men wore masks to obscure their identity except for Tex Howard, who chose not to, as it obscured his vision.

The robbers forced the store owner to open the safe at gunpoint. However, the outlaws were dismayed when they quickly discovered that the payroll had not yet arrived. Left with no other options, they looted everything that was in the safe. The robbers took some cash and a watch and then robbed all of the employees and customers in the store.

Meanwhile, several citizens outside recognized that a robbery was in progress and confronted the two cowboy lookouts waiting near the door.

When J.C. Tappenier exited the Bon Ton Saloon next door, they ordered him to go back in. He refused, and the robbers killed him with a single shot to the head. Cochise County deputy sheriff D. Tom Smith was having supper with his wife across the street at the Bisbee House. He ran out into the street, and the robbers ordered him to go back inside. Smith refused and told them he was an officer of the law. One of the bandits reportedly said, "Then you are the one we want!" and immediately shot him. The deputy was killed instantly, and his body fell beneath a freight wagon on the street. Another local man, known only as "Indian Joe," was wounded in the leg as he frantically tried to escape the shooting. Annie Roberts, who was pregnant, heard the commotion and went to the door of the Bisbee House restaurant to see what was going on. The robbers fired multiple shots in her direction. Roberts was shot, the bullet shattering her spine and mortally wounding her. John A. Nolly, a local freighter, was standing near his wagon when he was shot in the chest. Roberts and Nolly died later that evening.

The robbers exited the store, and they all ran for their horses, firing at anyone they saw along the way. Deputy Sheriff William "Billy" Daniels had just left his saloon when he heard the gunfire. He emptied his revolver at the fleeing outlaws but missed. The whole crime lasted less than five minutes, and with cash secured, the bandits left the town at a leisurely pace, evidently unworried about capture. The robbers rode over Mule Pass and out of the city. East of Bisbee, at a place called Soldier's Hole, they divided the money and went their separate ways.

A telegraph was sent to Sheriff J.L. Ward in Tombstone and he quickly formed two posses. He led one himself, while the other was under the watchful eye of Deputy Sheriff William Daniels.

When Daniels arrived in Bisbee, he began to question its citizens, including John Heath, who was at his saloon. Heath told Deputy Daniels that he knew some of the men who were involved and volunteered his assistance in helping to find them. The posse departed, with Heath leading the way. However, the lawmen found nothing and soon accused Heath of leading them on a false trail.

The posse continued to search for the outlaws and eventually found all five men. They were all brought back to Tombstone for questioning.

During their interrogation, some of the outlaws began to suggest that John Heath was the mastermind behind the robbery. As a result, the authorities brought Heath in for further questioning. Under pressure, Heath eventually confessed to having prior knowledge of the crime. He was arrested and jailed with the other outlaws.

Haunted Tombstone

On February 17, the trial for the five killers began, and two days later, they were all sentenced to be hanged on March 8, 1884.

Heath's trial began on February 20, and he admitted to being the mastermind of the robbery because the others lacked the intelligence. However, he insisted that the killings were never a part of the plan and that he was not responsible for the murders committed by the other five men. The next day, Heath was convicted of second-degree murder and conspiracy to commit robbery and sentenced to life in the Yuma prison.

The citizens of Bisbee were outraged, and a mob of fifty men soon gathered. Led by a man named Mike Shaughnessy, they descended on the Tombstone jail on the morning of February 22. The mob took Heath down Toughnut Street and lynched him from a telegraph pole at the corner of First and Toughnut Streets. In his last moments, he said, "I have faced death too many times to be disturbed when it actually comes." As the rope began to pull him skyward, he cried out one last request, "Don't mutilate my body or shoot me full of holes!" Public approval of the lynching could be seen in records of his official cause of death: "We the undersigned, a jury of inquest, find that John Heath came to his death from emphysema of the lungs—a disease common in high altitudes—which might have been caused by strangulation, self-inflicted or otherwise."

It is hard to say that what people have claimed to have seen is actually the ghost of John Wesley Heath, as there are not enough details to make a definite connection. However, something odd has been happening near this intersection for quite some time. On March 19, 1898, the *Arizona Daily Star* ran a story about Tombstone titled "A Nice Place for Ghosts":

> *Tombstone has again got up some excitement, this time on account of a haunted house, wherein spooks appear to have a gay old time and make as much noise as the ambitious daughter of a next door neighbor learning to play the piano. A few nights ago a miner who was riding horseback past the house heard unusual noises. He thought he heard footsteps behind him, but on looking backward discovered nothing. His horse became frightened at some object, and trembling with fear ran at full speed down the hill and could not be induced to go back.*
>
> *The* Star *does not usually take a controlling interest in the capital stock of ghost stories, but if there are such things as ghosts, they couldn't find a nicer, quieter place to play than at Tombstone.*

Haunted Tombstone

Tombstone's local newspaper, the *Epitaph*, has published several stories over the years about the ghostly happenings that occur around the town. Some are tongue-in-cheek, while others tell of more harrowing stories.

The *Tombstone Epitaph*, 1880s—that ghost again:

> *Strange some people can't even be decent after they are dead, but must go prancing around the country in their night robes disturbing the peace of the community. Before day, yesterday morning, this disconsolate spirit that has been seen on several occasions paid a visit to the vicinity of Second and Bruce, and disturbed the slumbers of some of the compositors of this office; one of them went to the door to get a drink of water and saw "his nibs" waltzing around over the stones just as if he was happy. Whether it was the ghost or the strangeness of the taste of the water, it is not known but the compositor turned around quickly and yelled to his companions and spilled his water all over the floor in the rapidity of his movements. His friends got to the door just in time to see the ghost making rapid strides for his home in the Boneyard close by.*
>
> *Notice is hereby given to that ghost to keep away from the vicinity mentioned beforehand for the residents are peaceful, hard working people and won't be bullied by a ghost, and the gentlemen might be made a lead mine of some time, for there are numerous guns in waiting. A word to the wise is sufficient.*

The *Tombstone Epitaph*, July 30, 1881—a perturbed spirit that walks Fremont Street:

> *As prosaic and matter of fact as most people are, when the subject of the Supernatural is broached, there is a vein of superstition very deep down beneath the surface in almost every heart which will crop out now and then, suppress it as they may. It is the aristocratic thing in almost every old house to have a grey or white Spectre that always appears to give warning of any abnormal event that is about to occur, and of late the more pretentious cities have their nocturnal visitants that are claimed to be of the other ethereal. It hardly comes within the Realms of possibility that so a new place as Tombstone should have developed a good sized ghost that can be seen only during the midnight hours, wandering aimlessly up and down on the north side of Fremont Street, between 6th and 7th. This statement coming to the ears of an* Epitaph *reporter, he was detailed*

Haunted Tombstone

to interview that gentleman whom it was reported has seen this denizen of the Realms of space and find out the true inwardness of this case. Upon approaching this gentleman, who is a well-known personage in Tombstone, he at first fought shy and made an effort to evade the subject, but upon pressing him for the facts of the mystery, if there were any, upon a solemn pledge of secrecy as to his name and residence, he told the following plain and straightforward story.

It happened in this wise: One evening he had been up to New Boston to see a lady friend and stayed rather late, say until nearly 12 o'clock, when he started for his home in the lower part of the city. All was black darkness and silence, save the occasional howl of a miserable cur in the neighborhood. Wrapped in pleasant meditations until he reached a point between 6th and 7th streets, he was startled by a soft, rustling sound upon his right, at the same moment his frame was penetrated by an unearthly chill, when involuntarily his head was turned to the right where he saw gliding along in close proximity the ghostly figure of a man about his own height clothed entirely in dark grey. It is unnecessary to affirm that his hair erected itself like "the quills upon the fretful porcupine." In his fright his gaze riveted upon his majesty until in an instant, and as mysterious as it appeared, this semblance of a man disappeared, vanished into *Thin Air.* There was no other sound other than the faint rustle already described, no sound of footfalls or other audible noise to indicate its presence. When freed from the hateful presence he quickened his pace and made rapid haste to his room, where, feeling the *Drowsy God* pressing his eyeballs down for sleep the activity of his mind drove away slumber until the first faint dawn to the east. Since then upon two similar occasions, he has seen the same mysterious visitant under precisely the same conditions, preceded by the soft rustling sound [of] an unearthly chill penetrating his body.

Upon being closely questioned he did not vary one iota from the facts as herein narrated and solemnly averred that he upon on each occasion duly in the possession of his scares. [sic] Before this, he had been a laughing skeptic upon the subject of the supernatural, but now he is as serious a believer in the possibility of perturbed souls manifesting themselves upon the scenes of their crimes or violent taking off as he was before a scoffer. He has no Theory as to which one of the aver, who has met a violent death in Tombstone, this silent Walker is, but insist that it is someone of them come back as a warning to evildoers whose acts will not bear an investigation in the light of day.

Haunted Tombstone

Another ghost story that takes place on Fremont Street involves the apparition of a woman in a white gown who has been seen near the street's intersection with Third Street. According to the stories, she is thought to have committed suicide after her child died of yellow fever in 1880. Her ghost has even been said to block traffic and has been reported as far as nine miles out of town.

A walk through the darkened streets of Tombstone can be an enriching experience. The town takes on a different flair that simply isn't there during the daylight hours. But be aware. You may not be alone.

BIBLIOGRAPHY

Books

Agnew, Jeremy. *Entertainment in the Old West: Theater, Music, Circuses, Medicine Shows, Prizefighting and Other Popular Amusements*. Jefferson, NC: McFarland, 2011.
Bruns, Roger. *Desert Honkytonk*. Golden, CO: Fulcrum Publishing, 2000.
Garcez, Antonio. *Arizona Ghost Stories*. Hanover, NM: Red Rabbit Press, 1998.
Goldstien, Diane, Sylvia Grider and Jeannie Thomas. *Haunting Experiences: Ghosts in Contemporary Folklore*. Logan: Utah State University Press, 2007.
Hawley, Joshua. *Tombstone's Most Haunted*. Tombstone, AZ: Tombstone Paranormal, 2009.
Ledoux, Gary. *Tombstone Tales: Stories from the Town Too Tough to Die...and Beyond*. Tombstone, AZ: Goose Flats Publishing, 2010.
Sobel, Bernard. *Burleycue: An Underground History of Burlesque*. New York: B. Franklin, 1932.

Websites

Ackerman, Rita. "Transcriptions and Research for the Article, 'Urban Legend'." Accessed August 10, 2017. http://ritaackerman.weebly.com/documents.html.
Big Nose Kate's Saloon. "History." Accessed August 19, 2017. http://bignosekates.info/history1.html.

Bibliography

Bob & Sharon's Travel Adventures. "Tombstone, AZ—04/14/15." Accessed August 12, 2017. https://casitacampers.blogspot.com/2015/04/tombstone-az-041415.html.

Davis, Carolyn. "The Old Bird Cage Theatre, Llewellyn Worldwide." Accessed August 14, 2017. http://www.llewellyn.com/journal/article/21.

Ferguson, Julie. "Buford House: Tombstone's Haunted B&B." Echoes of the Southwest. Accessed August 10, 2017. http://www.echoesofthesouthwest.com/2010/05/buford-house-tombstones-haunted-b.html.

Find a Grave. "James C. 'Justice Jim' Burnett." Accessed November 28, 2017. https://www.findagrave.com/cgi-bin/fg.cgi?page=gr&GRid=19436730.

Hall, Ashley. "Boot Hill Cemetery Ghost Photo." The Paranormal Guide. Accessed November 4, 2017. http://www.theparanormalguide.com/blog/boot-hill-cemetery-ghost-photo.

Hawley, Joshua. "Buford House." Tombstone Paranormal Investigations. Accessed August 10, 2017. http://www.spiritsoftombstone.com/storiesbuford.html.

Historical Marker Project. "Cambell & Hatch Saloon and Billiard Parlor." Accessed November 15, 2017. http://www.historicalmarkerproject.com/markers/HMWPF_campbell-hatch-saloon-and-billiard-parlor_Tombstone-AZ.html.

Janice. "Tears on Their Tombstones." *Tombstone Times* (June 2005). Accessed September 10, 2017. http://www.tombstonetimes.com/stories/tears.html.

Julie. "The Legend of Gold Dollar." Echoes of the Southwest. Accessed 12, 2107. http://www.echoesofthesouthwest.com/2010/07/legend-of-gold-dollar.html.

Kath. "The Birdcage Theater, Tombstone, Arizona." Rootsweb. Accessed July 13, 2017. http://archiver.rootsweb.ancestry.com/th/read/FOLKLORE/2000-10/0970726113.

Library of Congress. "*Tombstone Epitaph*, August 20, 1887, Image 3." Accessed June 9, 2017. http://chroniclingamerica.loc.gov/lccn/sn95060905/1887-08-20/ed-1/seq-3.

McClure, Rosemary. "The Spirit of Tombstone." *LA Times*. Accessed November 1, 2017. http://www.latimes.com/travel/la-tr-tombstone30oct30-story.html.

McGahey, Terry. "The Brunckow Cabin—The Bloodiest Cabin in Arizona." American Cowboy Chronicles. Accessed September 18, 2017. http://www.americancowboychronicles.com/2016/06/the-brunckow-cabin-bloodiest-cabin-in.html.

Bibliography

Moran, Mark. "Bird Cage Theatre." Weird Arizona. Accessed September 12, 2017. http://www.weirdus.com/states/arizona/ghosts/bird_cage_theatre.

Nagle, Dutch. "Bloodiest Cabin in Arizona History." *Herald/Review Media*. Accessed September 18, 2017. http://www.myheraldreview.com/news/bloodiest-cabin-in-arizona-history/article_b5ede040-fdc9-11e5-97e2-37e73bf6f789.html.

National Park Service. "Tombstone." National Register of Historic Places Inventory. Accessed June 24, 2017. https://npgallery.nps.gov/pdfhost/docs/NHLS/Text/66000171.pdf.

PINCURLADMIN. "Burlesque Haunts—The Bird Cage Theater." Pin Curl. Accessed July 13, 2017. http://pincurlmag.com/burlesque-haunts-the-bird-cage-theater.

Shaw, Sandy. *Ghosts, Phantoms in the Desert—Desert USA*. Accessed August 12, 2017. https://www.desertusa.com/desert-arizona/haunted-deserts.html.

Sierra Nevada Airstreams. "The Bird Cage Theatre Story." Accessed July 13, 2017. http://sierranevadaairstreams.org/memories/history/peewee/airstreams/as-trailers/birdcage-story.pdf.

Tito412. "Poked at the Birdcage Theater." Your Ghost Stories. Accessed August 12, 2017. http://www.yourghoststories.com/real-ghost-story.php?story=12326.

Tombstone Travel Tips. "Boothill in the 1880s." Accessed November 3, 2017. http://www.tombstonetraveltips.com/boothill.html.

Trimble, Marshall. "Antics at the Bird Cage Theater." *True West Magazine*. Accessed 12, 2017. https://truewestmagazine.com/antics-at-the-bird-cage-theater.

U.S. Gen Web Archives. "JAMES C. BURNETT, July 8, 1897, *Arizona Republican* Newspaper." Accessed November 28, 2017. http://files.usgwarchives.net/az/cochise/obits/burnett.txt.

Weiser, Kathy. "Haunted Tombstone." Legends of America. Accessed August 19, 2017. http://www.legendsofamerica.com/az-tombstoneghosts4.html.

Wikipedia. "Billy Claiborne." Accessed August 12, 2017. https://en.wikipedia.org/wiki/Billy_Claiborne.

———. "The Bird Cage Theatre." Accessed July 13, 2017. https://en.wikipedia.org/wiki/Bird_Cage_Theatre.

———. "Bisbee Massacre." Accessed August 12, 2017. https://en.wikipedia.org/wiki/Bisbee_Massacre.

———. "Buckskin Frank Leslie." Accessed August 12, 2017. https://en.wikipedia.org/wiki/Franklin_Leslie.

Bibliography

———. "Luke Short." Accessed August 12, 2017. https://en.wikipedia.org/wiki/Luke_Short#Duel_with_Jim_Courtright.

———. "Morgan Earp." Accessed August 12, 2017. https://en.wikipedia.org/wiki/Morgan_Earp.

———. "O.K. Corral (Building)." Accessed July 7, 2017. https://en.wikipedia.org/wiki/O.K._Corral_(building).

———. "Tombstone, Arizona." Accessed 12, 2017. https://en.wikipedia.org/wiki/History_of_Tombstone.

———. "Virgil Earp." Accessed November 28, 2017. https://en.wikipedia.org/wiki/Virgil_Earp.

Newspapers

"All I Know, I Have Been Living with Her." Cochise County Coroner's Inquests, August 17, 1888, Arizona Department of Library, Archives and Public Records.

Arizona Daily Star. "Specter Sport." November 2, 2005.

Arizona Republic. "Cross the Bridge and Hear the Phantoms Shriek." September 23, 1979.

Daily Tombstone. February 19, 1886.

Hunter, H.S. "Nameless. More Dust and Bones." *El Paso Herald Reporter*, April 6, 1933.

———. "News Writers Elegy and Boot Hill Cemetery." *Tombstone Epitaph*, April 4, 1928.

San Bernardino County Sun. "Bird Cage Theater in Arizona Wrecked." September 18, 1931.

Tom, Correa. "Leslie's Luck." *Tombstone Epitaph*, November 18, 1882.

Tombstone Epitaph. April 18, 1933.

———. "Ghosts: Apparitions Make for Business Bucks." January 26, 2007.

———. "The Grand Hotel." September 9, 1880.

———. "Morgan Earp Shot Down and Killed While Playing Billiards." Accessed November 15, 2017. http://www.tombstone1880.com/archives/morgan.htm.

Tombstone Weekly Epitaph. "A Disgraceful Scene." May 3, 1890.

About the Author

Cody Polston is a historian who enjoys giving tours of Albuquerque and other historic sites in the American Southwest. He has appeared on numerous radio and television programs, including *Dead Famous* (Biography Channel), *Weird Travels* (Travel Channel) and *In Her Mother's Footsteps* (Lifetime Channel exclusive), as well as *Extreme Paranormal* and *The Ghost Prophecies* (both A&E network). Cody is the author of four books on paranormal topics, the host and producer of the popular podcast *Ecto Radio* and the writer for *Ghosthunter X* magazine. He is the founder of the Southwest Ghost Hunters Association and has been investigating paranormal claims since 1985.

Visit us at
www.historypress.com